Your Soul's Companion

Dear Art,

Hope you enjoy the book.

Wendy

"This Mandala, dedicated on 1/23/2012,
joyously brings forth a jewel in a lotus,
surrounded by the elements and all living things on Earth in their life cycles,
watched over by the Eye of the Universe, with the Blessings of God. "

Made with love by: Patrick, Sou, and Milan

Photograph by Carlton SooHoo, Panospin Studios

Your Soul's Companion

tools and tales for your spiritual journey

Wendy Marks

with Susan Spector

Wolfmarks

www.yoursoulscompanion.com
www.wendymarks.com

ISBN: 978-1493546916
Printed in USA

Art & Design

INTERIOR

Mandala
Original Mosaic by Patrick Hsiung, Sou Chu, and Milan Stanic

Labyrinth Illustrations
Susan Spector

All Other Illustrations
Patrick Hsiung

Interior Design
Susan Spector, David Spector

COVER

Crystal Orb
Original Photograph by Jean Davis
Crystal Energy Images

Cover Art and Design
Cammy Broadhurst

Wolfmarks Logo
Patrick Hsiung

To

Chonyi Richard Allen
who not only saw the path ahead of me
but gently pushed me onto it

Susan Spector
my partner on this odyssey
It would not have happened without you

And, as always, to my brother
Keith David Marks, 1957- 2006
I miss you every day

Contents

PART ONE

"I'm Spiritual, Not Religious"

PART TWO

Cornerstones of a Spiritual Practice

PART THREE
Life in the Balance

PART FOUR
Being Human

Acknowledgements

Many people have lent their support to the creation of this book. A few, however, have been instrumental in bringing it to fruition: David Spector, for the assistance given both to me and Susan, and for his balanced view of things; Patrick Hsuing, for his wonderful images that reveal a new way of looking at ancient concepts; Jean Davis, for her wonderful art and vision; Judy Kogut-O'Connell, for her support, energy and wisdom; Donna Platt, for always having my back; Sou Chu, who was great at testing out ideas; Tim Gilman, for his cyber know-how; Karen Shaw, who always knew I could do it; and Ray Edwards, for great marketing expertise.

Many thanks also to all my early readers: Sou Chu, Dwayne Gilman, Jerry Kantor, Kathleen Johnston Cross, Ray Edwards, David Spector, Donna Platt and Judy Kogut-O’Connell. Your advice helped fine tune the work and make it ready to meet the world.

Sincere thanks to all of my clients for sharing their journeys with me.

Introduction

I found myself standing at a crossroads. I was adrift, having experienced several significant losses. I felt unsure, afraid and confused about my future. I decided to ask God to give me a sign, even though I wasn't sure there was a God. I found myself saying, "Give me a sign. Show me something that gives me an indication of what I need to be doing with my life now. I'd really like some specific instructions, God. I've been winging it on my own for a long time. This would be a really good time to give me some help."

And I sat, never really believing that some infinite being would pay any attention to my confusion or distress. After all, I was certain that God had much bigger fish to fry.

Then the phone rang...

So began my current career, embracing and using my innate intuitive gifts. By surrendering to the answer I received so many years ago, I was able to fulfill my life's purpose to help others find their spiritual path and heal themselves along the way. Perhaps you have been at a similar juncture, or simply want to expand your human experience on this earth. You may have a business plan, a ten-year goal or a retirement account, but without a plan for your inner life, you may feel that something's missing. If you are curious about beginning a spiritual practice and want practical, applicable tools and techniques, your journey begins here.

This book contains the message and the promise that you can transform your awareness and presence as a spiritual inhabitant of Earth. Within its pages, you will find a gentle and accessible handbook, a soul's companion. It contains the first steps on the path, steps that can begin a ripple effect, benefitting everything you do and all of your relationships, including our collective dream of world peace. After all, we must begin with ourselves.

This book has been buried inside of me for decades. It took a long time for me to find what I could authentically add to the discourse about spirituality. Thank you, reader, for embarking on this journey with me. And additional thanks go to the many wonderful folks who encouraged me to bring this project to fruition. This book is for people who have felt called to do more, to become more united with the Universe and to "heal the earth" in some way. If you've heard that little voice in your head and wondered, "Where do I begin?" then this book is for you. It is a starting point for a journey that will awaken your senses and light up your life, all without leaving your living room.

Does that sound dramatic? Impossible? Once you have read this book, you will know that the most mind-altering experience does not come from something that you swallow or smoke, but rather from your own mind, spirit and soul. My purpose is to provide you with useful tools to give you a greater understanding of both the inner workings of our own minds, souls and bodies, and how they relate to the outer world. I believe that we all have a path to follow and that path includes the promise of leaving the world a better place than when we entered it.

Inside This Book

This book is meant as a jumping-off point, not in any way excluding other works or differing views on its topics. It's my method of teaching basic spiritual practice, a method I have used with people of various educational, spiritual and cultural backgrounds and it appears to work almost universally.

Those who have worked with me in Spiritual Awakening will recognize my methods and manner of working. For new readers I've tried to present information in a way that both makes sense and is approachable to the novice and mid-level practitioner.

The first section sets the stage with a discussion of a more inclusive view of religion in order to honor and reflect upon the world's traditions while we grow toward a spiritual path of our choosing. You will hear about my own journey (including what happened after the phone rang). Next, we'll discover your wonderful energy body, the aura and the chakras (energy centers) and how they relate to your physical, emotional, mental and spiritual being. We'll introduce guides and teachers, both those in the spirit world of our imagination and the "real-life" teachers who share their wisdom. Lastly, we'll look at the many types of intuitive and psychic abilities. Here, you may find gifts you are already using, or perhaps are holding back because of confusion or even apprehension.

The second part contains the cornerstones of a spiritual practice. Once you set your intention for the highest good, we'll work toward creating a private, sacred space in which to meditate and feel safe. Learning to protect yourself from negativity in the world and removing draining connections to others will liberate you from holding onto harmful energy. Meditation techniques and tips help you to center and calm, all held in the life-giving power of the breath. Finally, we are introduced to deep listening, the kind that connects us to our highest self and truest expression of the Divine.

Part Three looks at essential topics that we must examine and question as we live toward the answers on our path. Good and evil, miracles and the life force itself call upon us to form a mature and ethical viewpoint and to put those values into practice.

In the last section, "Being Human," we revisit, armed with new tools and awareness, the toughest life challenges of negative emotions and the things over which we have no control. It's a loving invitation to meet these difficulties, and surrender to the invaluable life lessons that they are. Coming full circle, we'll embrace the vitality of the moment, wherein lies the secret to living life fully. Our higher self tells us that we always have a choice to live in the present, the space that contains Everything: the eternal Now.

Throughout the book are stories from my life and practice as a Medical Intuitive and spiritual teacher. I hope you'll find them informative and sometimes humorous. Also included are many exercises that will help you experience and integrate the information you have learned. They are meant to be enjoyable and easy, yet when practiced over time, they are powerful tools that will "grow" you and serve you all of your life. May it be so.

About Me

Who am I to write this book? I have been psychic and a medium all my life. I remember my shock at realizing that other people could not feel what their friends, parents and siblings were feeling. I was confused when people did hurtful or inconsiderate things. Couldn't they "feel" the damage they caused, or the joy, the feeling of making someone happy or understood? Was there anything like it? I literally felt joy come back to me as I tuned in to someone's pleasure and happiness. I felt sad when people were casually hurt, especially when it could have been avoided.

The discovery of my particular gifts occurred when I was two years old. My grandmother, who lived in New York like the rest of the clan, was in Boston getting treatment for her diabetes. In my mind, I saw her getting on a plane and saw the plane crash. I climbed up on a kitchen chair, took down the pinned-up phone number of her hotel, called my Nana, and told her not to take the plane. She changed planes. The first plane actually did crash because of birds flying into the engine. When Nana arrived home, she calmly walked over to me, kissed the top of my head and said to my mother "I guess she has IT." That's what we called psychic ability in my family--IT. But I didn't have a clue how to use IT. It would take me many years and a few bumps to figure IT out.

As my life progressed, I realized that I was different. I could not successfully compete in sports or any activity requiring any significant gross motor skills, but I had abilities to see the future, feel many things and to help people heal.

Many people in my family were similarly gifted and they went on to use their skills in many wonderful ways. But they stayed "in the closet." The possibility of ridicule or rejection was too difficult to face and I understood this well. I remember once waiting for a chiropractic appointment with my small daughter. The chiropractor displayed my Medical Intuitive business cards in his office as a courtesy to me. When the receptionist announced my name, a man jumped up and began screaming at me that I preyed on innocent people. We had never met, and he had no knowledge of me or my skills. I can only assume he had been wronged by someone and was taking it out on me. My daughter, always a brave soul, was the first to recover from the assault. She walked up to him and said "Don't yell at my mommy!" So it's quite understandable to me why my family did not wish to "come out." However, they used their skills as teachers, doctors and therapists, mainstreaming their gifts in traditional ways.

My path was different. I went on to train in traditional helping fields although it did not really work the way I thought it would. I always knew I'd land in a helping profession. It was in my bones. Even as a child, I would tell my parents and friends what was wrong with them, often in inappropriate ways. I was an amateur. Often, I did not understand the gravity of what I said or the possible impact of saying it. I felt inadequate to deal with my "gifts" and often saw them as a curse. This perception led to many years of denial and frustration. I knew there was a better way; I just didn't know what it was.

I worked in many traditional areas: as a therapist, non-profit administrator, geriatric care manager and director of an educational collaborative and more. I enjoyed all of this work, but I secretly used my knowledge as a Medical Intuitive to determine what was wrong with someone. I might say something like "Gee, you should get a mammogram, it's been a while," if I suspected cancer or "You look like you are having stomach discomfort." Over time, I came to realize that this situation wasn't working because it's very important to base any relationship, therapeutic or otherwise, on honesty. I was very torn and I struggled a great deal.

Eventually, I received training that enabled me to use my gifts appropriately, and I now can help others with similar abilities to sort out what their gifts are and to make appropriate use of them.

About All of Us

The Chinese have a saying (that is actually a curse): "May you live in interesting times." In fact, we do live in interesting times. These times are dangerous and wonderful, and, I believe, unique in the history of humankind. We have the chance, and the choice, to make a difference, to be the people who save the planet or the people who ignore all signs and warnings and watch the world continue to deteriorate.

You might ask "How can getting in touch with myself, learning about spirituality, or meditating daily change the planet?" We have to start somewhere. We have to start by cleaning up our own act. Unfortunately, my generation, the Baby Boomers, will be leaving the world to the next generation with an impossible repair mission. The very least we can do is make an effort to reverse some of the seemingly inexorable damage that we've done. The place to start is within ourselves.

Sometimes, I feel as though we've made a full circle back to the late '60s. It was always true that "what goes around comes around." It was true that one needs to think globally in order to act locally. And it is still true; it can change the world, one person at a time. Each small step that we make toward enlightenment furthers our understanding of ourselves and therefore begins the process of shifting our planet from darkness to light. If we change our world view, we teach that to our children. If we change our world view, we teach that to our parents. The only way that change can occur is person by person.

The only way I personally know how to change the world is by teaching what I know to be true, in order to move things toward the Light. That light is the spirit within ourselves, the light that shines from our eyes when we do something kind and wonderful. It's the very best in us.

We do indeed live in interesting times. Whether or not you believe in the apocalyptic visions regarding the End of Days, Mayan prophecy, or the I Ching, we have all heard "doom and gloom" presentations about our impending demise: if the Rapture or something similar happens, we'll all be caught unaware, except for those who believe in that prophecy. I myself prefer to take a positive attitude about the whole thing and assume that we are going to survive, and do the best I can to ensure that there is a planet for us to survive in.

We face the reality of a changing planet because of our poor stewardship. Some things we can change, and some things we cannot. It's too late for us to stop climate change but if we get wise, we can probably slow it down. I don't know about you, but I despair for my children and possible future grandchildren. I really want to empower you. I really want you to feel and know that you have some control, not only of your personal destiny, but you can also affect the destiny of the planet if you work with the Light.

My own journey has led me to teach those who seek a path to their better selves, to turn on the lights of Light Beings. That light exists within all of us; it is our job to find out what the nature of that light is and to follow that light down our path. Whether you walk that path as a Jew, Buddhist, Muslim or Jain, or as an agnostic seeking answers, to *not* walk that path is perhaps a greater risk. Isn't it better to explore than to hide in the trenches? Isn't it better to be a curious monkey than a hiding ostrich?

"...he not busy being born is busy dying."

BOB DYLAN

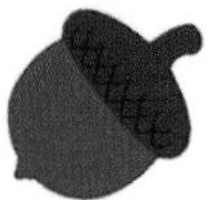

PART ONE

"I'm Spiritual, Not Religious."

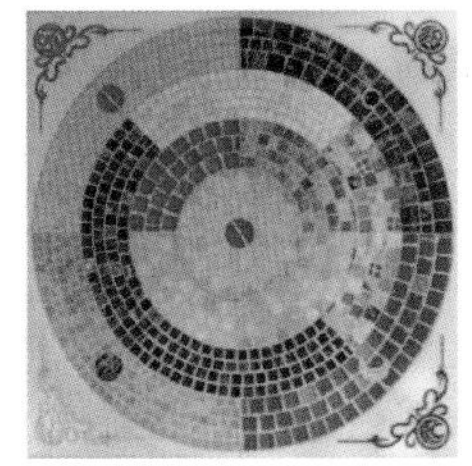

CHAPTER ONE

A Path of Your Own

Religion: Awareness and Choice

Many of us are no longer comfortable with the spiritual path that we were assigned or perhaps we did not receive a good introduction to a spiritual path from our parents. Our religious initiation may have felt obligatory and devoid of spirituality, a part of our childhood but nothing that we could hold onto as a path forward. When I say "devoid" I don't mean that there was no value to it, but rather that it may not have been deemed as important an issue in the way that, say, our hygiene or our work ethic was.

The upbringing many of us had was a secular version of the religious observations of our parents. We grew up outside of defined communities, often in the wasteland of suburbia, where everyone did their own thing behind closed doors, rather than as an integral community. For the first time, families scattered all over the world and the "nuclear" family became a very short-term experience. Whether this diaspora was caused by divorce, education, employment or other reason, families met only for occasions, rather than daily or weekly. We drifted farther and farther apart geographically and emotionally. While this can be beneficial in some respects, it also meant that our religious or spiritual "glue" became unstuck. We didn't go to the church of our fathers and grandfathers. We felt open to explore other types of worship.

When I was in college, I had a roommate who had been brought up a traditional Catholic, then went to a Quaker high school. Together we did something we called "survey religion." Each week, we would go to a different community to worship. It was wonderful. I remember the heady feeling of freedom that all religions were open for me to explore. We went to traditional mosques, Orthodox Jewish temples, Greek Orthodox churches, Catholic masses, Congregational meetings, whatever we felt interested us that week. I especially liked the Quaker Meeting, where, instead of a pre-determined service led by clergy, individuals spoke only when moved to do so. "Survey religion" was, for us, a fascinating journey that began the opening of my mind to other religious concepts and beliefs. Like many others, I somehow felt that my religious experience was incomplete and that other religions and ideas filled in the gaps. I think this kind of broadening of knowledge has created society's openness to new ways of thinking about spirituality and one's personal path.

Whether for better or worse, many people now look for religion in a different form. We seek religion that's tailored to our personal wants and desires and meets our individual needs. I think that is an extraordinarily good idea. I don't see any reason we should all fit into a cookie-cutter version. This idea is actually a concept of the new spiritual model as I see it: that we can choose a tailored path that fits the unique way in which we may benefit the world. This path can be found in many communal settings, or it can be found within individuals seeking enlightenment on their own. There's also the issue of style: some people long for the monastic life, others for group experiences. Our personalities inform whether or not we choose, for example, to read this book or something that is more mainstream. Instead of there being 4,546 religions and sects that divide up the world, we now appear to be putting together our own personal view of the Divine. (I work with a shaman who was raised a Taiwanese Buddhist, then converted to Christianity, then became a Unitarian).

We can choose a tailored path that fits the unique way in which we may benefit the world.

The days when we assumed we would raise our children in the same religion that our parents raised us likely have passed. We could talk at great length about whether this is a good or bad thing, but it's true nonetheless. And if you are reading this book, I assume that you wish to walk a path of your own choosing. Or, perhaps you are choosing the path that your parents chose, but you opt to dance down the path instead of walk. I believe our paths are to a great degree strongly indicated by our nature and intuition. We then elect to take whatever side roads we desire as we continue down that path. The way that we dress for that path, prepare for that path and follow the signs on that path is individual.

Because each of us needs to come to our own definition of the Divine, throughout this book I use the terms "God," "spiritual," "He" and "She" and many others that may be considered interchangeable. The intention of this book is to be inclusive and not limit our experience of the Divine.

Teachers of Timeless Wisdom

Each of us can now choose a teacher, a wise one who shows us what we need to do and how to do it with grace, candor and integrity, the one who gives us an outline to follow but does not tell us what to write. We can then move on from that teacher and continue down our path, dancing to the beat of our own music. This is the way of the future of belief as I and many others see it.

My training was with a shaman and therefore I share with you from that perspective. Shamanism is an ancient form of accessing the unknown, using elders and others as guides, to further growth and enlightenment. Although not easily available as a reference point in this century, the idea of a shaman, a wise one, a crone or a magician lives within all of us as an archetype. An archetype is a universal concept like those we see in tarot cards and greeting cards: the wise grandmother, the wicked witch, the brave knight, the damsel in distress. These teachers have historically been individuals who helped us live through difficult times and life passages with grace, helped us transition from conception to birth, from life to death and just about everything in between. They offer us the opportunity for tradition and ritual, not unlike that which is offered to us by mainstream religions.

The difference between these more traditional teachers and other religious leaders is that the role of the shaman is often highly individual. It is often a reflection of a specific time or place. However, over the centuries, and all over the globe, the shaman's role has remained the same: as intermediaries between the worlds, helping to integrate the body, mind and spirit.

The modern shaman takes the timeless wisdom and applies its principles to contemporary needs. You will find that the ideas and exercises in this book can benefit those on any path, and that even if you are spiritual and religious, you still need the fundamental lessons herein to ground and protect yourself, to understand your gifts, your energy body and your intention as a blossoming spiritual being.

You may very well end up choosing your religion of birth, but it will be a voluntary choice, not an assignment. You'll eventually need a teacher, whether that person is a sage, crone or minister, but you can begin the process with a better understanding and a deeper knowing of what is in store for you and how to begin your walk toward "the great unknown."

So may I open your eyes to new possibilities and new ideas? Will I encroach on your religious beliefs, whatever they are? Allow me to share with you my concept of the religions of the world.

Many Gates to the City

I have, over the course of my half-century, studied many religious systems and beliefs. I have found good and truth and joy in all of them. For many years, I described myself as a "Jewbu," a person who had the Jewish belief system but practiced many of the Buddhist tenets and although I still consider myself a practicing Jew, that doesn't mean that I believe any other system is less valid—far from it. One winter, while I spent time at "Hindu boot camp" studying the Vedanta (ancient philosophical texts of India), my swami kept insisting that I choose the deity who was to be "my" deity, someone whose path I would use as a model for my own and would be my gateway to the Divine. I told her that I did not want to choose a deity or take a deity's name and that I preferred to remain inclusive and allow all of the deities to give me whatever information they chose to deliver. She said that was much more advanced than my current level of study, but finally let me be. It's interesting to note that contained in the Vedas is the statement "Truth is one, sages call it by various names."

Many of us today are allowing wisdom and inspiration to enlighten us from varied sources, performing our own "survey religion." One particular gentleman came to me to begin shamanic studies. His background in Catholicism left him with some uncomfortable ideas and feelings, although he longed for the spirituality of his childhood: the loving priest, the wise nuns and the gentle words of many of his teachers. He had become, however, uncomfortable about the church's stand on women, birth control and other issues. He felt like "a man without a country." He was certainly a man without a spiritual country.

This very intelligent and articulate man longed for something to believe in outside of himself. He felt the void of having no belief system in which to immerse himself. He wanted to feel part of a larger community, to feel a connection with the Universal, to have a relationship with the Divine. He wanted to be able to process his emotions and contextualize them in a spiritual way. In other words, he wanted what most of us want: a spiritual homeland, a spiritual country. At first he studied Tai Chi and other forms of martial arts. These arts gave him discipline to meditate and to practice, and were very useful to him, but in itself were not enough. On his journey with me, he explored the Hindu belief system and is currently studying Tibetan Buddhism. He is broadening his own spiritual vocabulary. It's amusing that in this process he asks me if it's okay to change his mind about what he believes or with whom he studies. I always tell him that the path is wonderful as long as it is satisfying his needs. Where he will end up I don't know, but his journey is beautiful and with each new piece of knowledge and each new method of study, he becomes a deeper, richer and more fulfilled human being.

"Truth is One, sages call it by various names."
—The Rigveda

It is through this man's journey that I came to the idea of a visual representation of my belief about the world's religions. The chorus I sing with sometimes performs gospel music, and one of the songs I really like is called "Twelve Gates to the City." The idea of the song, if you're not familiar with it, is that there are many ways to enter Jerusalem: three gates in the North, three gates in the South, three gates in the East, and three gates in the West. When I studied the concept, I decided that it was a Judeo/Christian/Muslim construct, not inclusive of all the other religions, so here is my image: imagine the Roman Colosseum, as if you were in a hot air balloon flying above it. You would see the central area, and on all sides, the many archways opening into it. Each of these archways goes to the same place, the central core of the Colosseum. Heaven, Nirvana, whatever we call it—that's what's in the center. So there are not just twelve gates to the city, but there are many, many gates. Whether you enter it from the point of a particular deity or just strolling through as a seeker, all gates lead to the Center.

CHAPTER TWO

One Teacher's Journey

Growing up Psychic

So how does a girl from Brooklyn come to be writing a book about spiritual studies? Well, I don't intend to write an autobiography, but a little background might help. I share my story so that if you see yourself in some of these situations, you'll have validation and a context to help you understand and accept your own gifts.

I mentioned that strong psychic abilities are prevalent in my family. My mother is clairvoyant and is also a medical intuitive, although she'd never admit that. My brother had incredible healing touch; he had "the hands." My cousin is able to see when people are lying, and so on. So I was blessed to be in a family where my gifts were not regarded as strange or abnormal. But I learned that acceptance at home would not help me in the outside world.

As a small child, I really didn't understand that other people did not "see" like me. I thought that everyone knew that the teacher was cranky because she had a terrible bellyache, that the kid sitting down the row from me had something wrong in her brain that turned out to be a tumor or that the girl down the hall had a big crack in her leg underneath that cast. I didn't realize that I wasn't normal—kids really don't. I didn't know this ability was unusual; I thought everyone was like me and knew these things. It was confusing.

At some point, I realized that this gift was confusing to other people and maybe a little scary. I think people were afraid that I could read their thoughts. I can't (and I'm very glad that I can't), but it's often assumed that if you have psychic abilities, you can hear what someone is thinking. That's not a gift that I would want to keep; that's a gift I would like to return!

When I was about nine years old, I went to a gypsy at a fair on Coney Island. I walked into her tent and there she was, garishly dressed with the typical large earrings and kholed eyes. I could tell she was bored and wondering what this child was doing in her tent. I handed her the requisite quarter and sat down on a rickety wooden stool. The light was dim. There were many candles and objects that I could not recognize that appeared very significant and exotic: a stuffed bird, a crystal ball, old leather books. She began to say things to me about my family and home. Then I could see her really look at me. She said, "Child, you are one of us. You must be very careful in your life and use your gift for good. You will be tempted to do harm, or act in anger, but that is not your way. You must be a healer. That is your destiny. Take me seriously, as I see into your soul." I ran from the tent. I was scared to death. Someone outside my family could see what I was! To this day, I wish I had stayed awhile and listened to her. Perhaps I could have avoided the confusion and difficulty of trying to be a square peg in a round hole.

Throughout my teens and my twenties, I alternated between thinking that I was being tortured and thinking that I had been given a great prize. One of the ways I made money in college was to volunteer for studies. I didn't volunteer for drug trials or other such medical studies, but I did volunteer for a lot of psychological studies. Someone had told one of the psychology graduate students that I was a psychic. Some trendy research was going on at that time. They gathered a bunch of people and gave us a series of tests to see how psychic we were. There were little cards with black symbols on them and I was supposed to tell the researcher what symbol was on the card.

This is when I realized you don't play with stuff you don't understand. These researchers were conducting exercises to increase my psychic ability, but not giving me any understanding or way to contextualize it. I started "seeing" fires, accidents on the highway, and all kinds of disasters. It was so disturbing that I had to pull out of the study. I almost had to drop out of school altogether. I couldn't stop seeing all of this suffering. I now understand why I saw the tragedies and not good things: negative vibrations and negative energies are very powerful, and strong pain, suffering and danger may radiate much more strongly, so instead of seeing, for example, the joy of a baby being born, I would see a car crash.

I think this experience set me back quite a bit, because for a number of years, I didn't talk about my abilities at all. I put them in the closet as best as I could and just allowed myself to use my "parking karma" (my ability to find a parking space whenever needed) and my signals of personal danger because they were practical to use. I stayed away from looking at anyone's body or using any of my other gifts. But I learned that suppressing your abilities in this way can actually cause physical harm and unfortunately, this period lasted for a while. I had the most disturbing dreams I've ever had in my life and I believe that was partly because I was not allowing my natural abilities to be used. I was exercising my muscles, though, for they were exercising themselves at night as I struggled in my bed.

Because I had always felt like a bit of a freak (outside of my home environment), I pursued a career that did not require me to be overt about my abilities. I became a rehabilitation counselor, combining psychotherapy and rehabilitation medicine (sort of a hybrid vehicle). I began to use my gifts again, but surreptitiously. People thought I had terrific diagnostic skills; they didn't know I was really "cheating." It wasn't until much later that I realized that looking at people without their permission is a really bad idea. It breaks all kinds of emotional, psychological, spiritual and other contracts, not to mention being a serious boundary violation. But I merrily went along, figuring out things that I wasn't supposed to know, and for the most part, helping people, until eventually, as is true with most cases of hubris, it would come back to haunt me. People who knew me were constantly asking me things like "You're looking at me funny. Did I say something wrong?" And I felt pretty out of control about the whole thing.

At the Crossroads

Years ago, I found myself at a crossroads in my life. I had just lost everything: my marriage, a business I had built from scratch and a business partner who was my dear friend and soul sister. I felt adrift. It was Erev Yom Kippur, the night before the holiest day of the Jewish year, the day in which what will happen in our upcoming year is written into the Book of Life. This is the night, so it is told, that God decides who lives, who dies and how they live and die. This is the night before the gates are closed at the end of the year, marking the beginning of the new year and all that we will encounter in the year to come: sickness, health, births, renewal and everything else.

I decided to sit on my back porch, light an illicit cigarette, and ask God to give me a sign. I had never been the type of person who would ask God to give me a sign. I wasn't even sure there *was* a God from whom to ask a sign. Yet here I was, completely at a loss; unsure, afraid, confused about my future, and about the livelihood I needed to support myself and my very young daughter. So I said to God, "Give me a sign, show me something that gives me an indication of what I need to be doing with my life now. And if you want me to serve you, spell it out for me please. I'd really like some specific instructions, God. I've been winging it on my own for a long time. This would be a really good time to give me some help."

Sometimes our path finds us.

So I sat, never really believing that some infinite being would pay any attention to my confusion or distress. After all, I'm sure that God had much bigger fish to fry. Then the phone rang.

My destiny was calling and it was with a woman's voice, from a Boston hospital's Neonatal Intensive Care Unit. I had no idea who she was, but clearly she was in great distress. When I asked how she got my name, she said that a friend of hers had told her that I was a medical intuitive. I had never called myself that. I wasn't even familiar with the term. She told me that her baby was dying. I was petrified. Talk about performance anxiety! I told her that I only knew about the anatomy and physiology of adults. I had never really tried to take a look at a baby. She begged me to do the best I could.

I asked her to nurse her son. As she held him to her breast, I was able to see him, much to my surprise. I immediately knew that he was suffering from several different infections, and I was told by a voice which antibiotics should be used for his recovery. I also told her to tell the doctors at the hospital that her cousin was a pediatrician, and that she had called her in California and gotten this advice. (I am quite conscientious about truthfulness, but in this case it seemed that, for once, the end did in fact justify the means. I knew that a big hospital would never accept my psychic diagnosis as prescriptive!) I was terrified. This was the big league. Real people were involved and people who weren't my family. Later that night, when the baby (who is now an adult) began to recover, I looked up and said to God, "Okay, you win. I guess that this is my path." Sometimes our path finds us.

What I really wanted God to say that evening was "Stick with your job. Work it out with your business partner. You have contributed a lot to human services and you deserve a business where you can both do well and do good. Hang in there, Wendy, and everything will be fine." It was not the answer I got.

Accepting "IT" All

By the time this change in my path occurred, I had entered my forties, and I was ready to begin again to look at IT all. I felt more secure about myself and my place in the world. I was able to take a clearer look at my abilities without feeling either afraid of them or terribly burdened by them. And that helped me a lot, because I realized that if you're given a gift, you're probably given it to use.

In order to understand myself better, I began working with a shaman. I didn't even know that's what he was called at that point. I studied with him more as a psychologically-trained counselor who had a spiritual orientation. But make no bones about it, he was, and still is, a shaman. I spent four years working with him. During that time, I needed to break down some of my preconceptions about myself and my place in the world and build up a new identity, including the responsibility of using my gifts.

Remember, I didn't always think of them as gifts. I used to joke with my family and say, "I wish there was a place like the one in Macy's where I can bring my gifts back and exchange them for something more useful, like being right-handed or being competent at sports." Times are more open now, but back then, people still thought of a fortune teller as the typical gypsy with the crystal ball and the turban, not some middle-aged lady in her home office with a cat.

I worked hard over those four years to break down preconceptions about people and about God. Some days, I really wondered if it was worth it to know myself and my relationship with the world. My teacher kept telling me that it was my responsibility to use my gifts. I fought that pretty hard for a long time and there were times when I still felt as if they were a burden, not a joy. But he persisted and patiently helped me to focus on the fact that I had actually been training all my life to become a medical intuitive. All of the jobs that I held, all of the things that I learned, prepared me and came together to help me use this ability.

My teacher told me I would write a book about the time that these events occurred. I told him that he was crazy. What would I write a book about? What could I possibly have to say that was unique or different, or would shed light on something that somebody else could do? I said, "Why don't you write a book?" He laughed, looked at me with that gleam in his eye and said, "Oh, you will write the book and it will help people to find their path."

I went on to find a way to become what he eventually called "a Unitarian of shamans." I am proud to be a Unitarian shaman. I think it allows me a greater breadth of work. I get to study different religions so that I can be knowledgeable for my students and clients and understand different orientations and concepts. And it's a lot more fun.

CHAPTER THREE

The Aura, the Chakras, and Your Energy Body

As we expand our awareness, we'll discover that we are more than the physical body: we are beings of energy, of light. This ancient knowledge is as true and as vital today as it ever was. Our spiritual education requires that we understand the "light body" we inhabit in this life and the ways we can keep it functioning in harmony with our highest good and with the world around us.

The Aura

The concept of the aura is prevalent in the popular media. From movies to TV shows, people talk about reading or perceiving the aura. Some of us are easily able to see auras and most of us can be trained to see them. Pictorial representations of the aura appear in virtually all religions. In pictures of many of the Hindu gods, they are surrounded by a halo. I believe that represents their aura. Jesus is often also represented with a halo around his head, possibly reflecting the concept of his aura. It is white golden light, the colors that are generally associated with God light. In much of the religious art of the past several centuries, significant saints and other important religious figures are shown with glowing light radiating from their bodies. Again, I believe their aura is represented this way.

An aura consists of light surrounding your energy body. Imagine that you are the yolk of an egg, your physical body represented by the yellow part. Your energy field or energy body would be the surrounding fluid around the yolk and the shell would be where your aura resides. Your aura surrounds you from above your head to below your feet, front and back. It is often viewed in various colors. If we are perfectly balanced physically, mentally, emotionally and spiritually, our aura might radiate the rainbow, from red all the way through the spectrum to violet. An aura can be used to learn a lot about a person. I can look at an aura before I even begin to assess a person's health and well-being and get a general idea of their mood, their physical health, and their mental state.

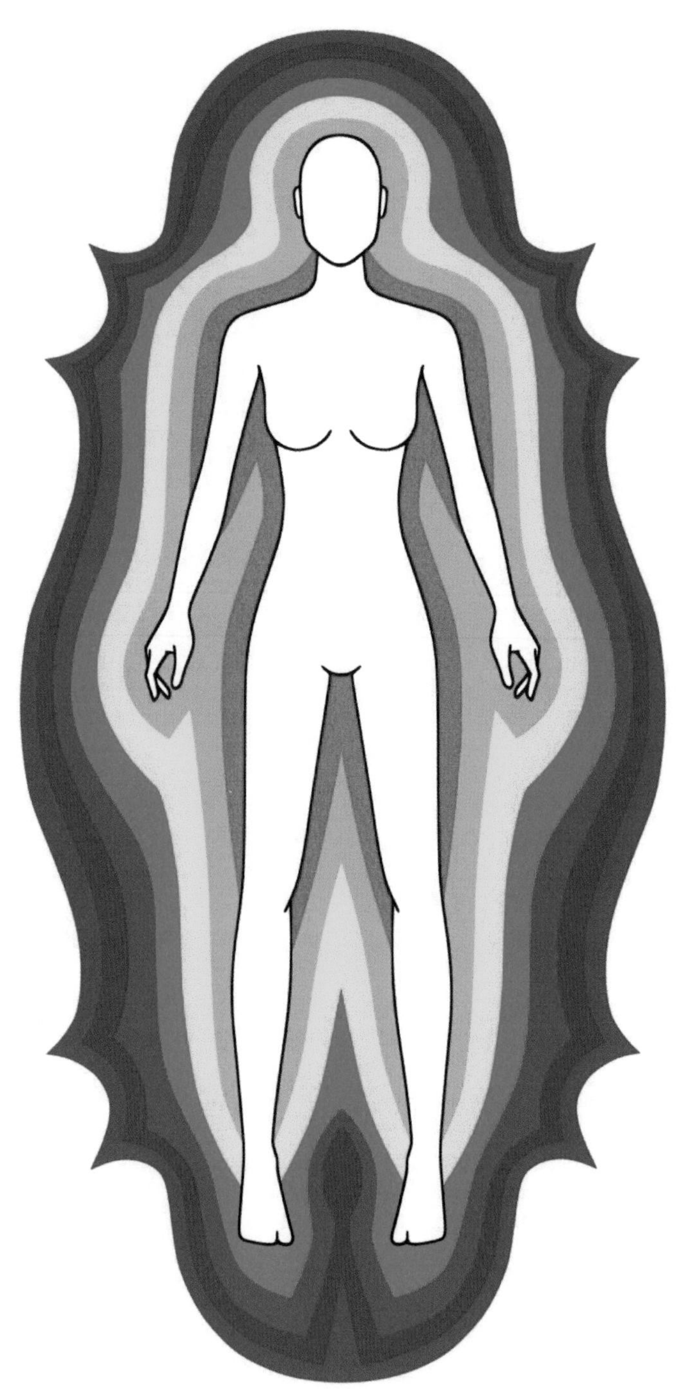

THE AURA

The aura is often described as rainbow-like, with layers of color. Sometimes I see it that way and other times I don't. If someone is very angry, I may actually see spiky red flames coming out of their energy body. In one class I taught where students paired off to read each other's auras, a woman saw bright red energy coming from a man's lower body and reaching out to her. When she described this, I had to determine whether it was sexual attraction or some form of aggression directed toward her. It turned out that neither of those things was the case. The man had just had a fight with someone in his family and was unable to control the energy coming out of his body.

It's worthwhile to try to look for auras. I think it's easier to see someone's aura with my eyes closed but it can be done with your eyes open as well. You may think that seeing auras is difficult to do. Let's try.

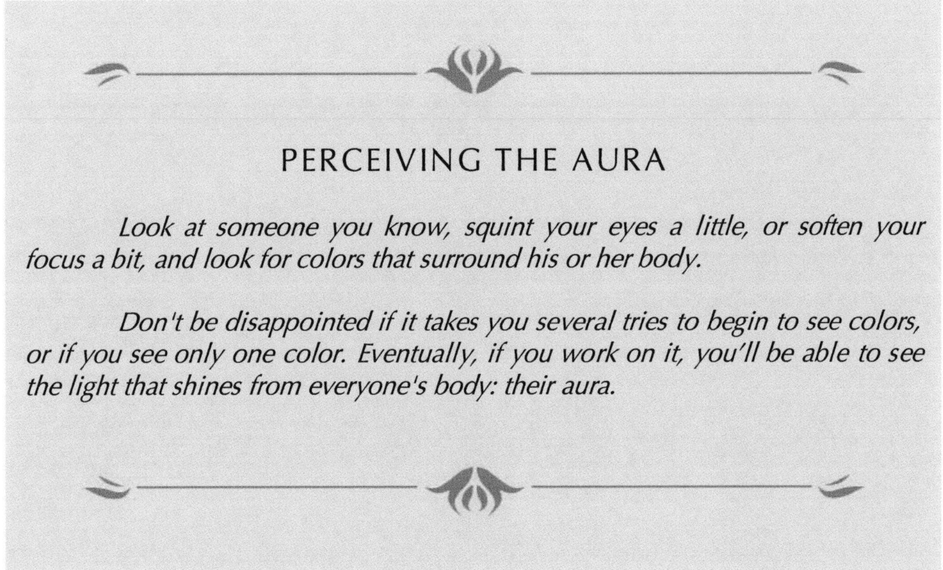

PERCEIVING THE AURA

Look at someone you know, squint your eyes a little, or soften your focus a bit, and look for colors that surround his or her body.

Don't be disappointed if it takes you several tries to begin to see colors, or if you see only one color. Eventually, if you work on it, you'll be able to see the light that shines from everyone's body: their aura.

The aura is important because it can give you so much information. Not everyone is a medical intuitive and not everyone is able to see the chakras. But with some work, most people are able to see auras. You may be able to see them but it may be happening without your conscious mind's awareness. I think the ability just takes a leap of trust and faith in your belief.

The Chakras

The concept of energy centers in the body has existed since humans first drew pictures of themselves. These energy centers are the chakras. I have seen drawings with as many as twenty-seven chakras in the body. For our purposes, we will look at the major seven.

Chakras are the seats of energy. Each chakra represents a different type of energy. For example, the heart chakra is what you might expect: the seat of the emotions of love and hate.

All of the chakras are shaped like funnels that go through your physical body. Did you ever play "telephone" with cups or cans when you were a kid? Picture two Dixie cups with a connecting string running from the front to the back of your body. Now imagine the Dixie cups are like flowers that can open and close. That image will give you a good idea of your chakras. People often forget that their chakras go through their bodies front to back. Because our eyes face forward and we tend to see what's in front of us, we sometimes forget. With the exception of the crown and the root, our chakras also go out the back. The ideas of "being stabbed in the back" or "back-biting" are representations of the fact that energy can harm us from the front and from the back, or for that matter, benefit us from the front and back.

Walking around in the world, your chakras should be partially open—open enough to receive information, but not wide open. If they are wide open, you are vulnerable to attack, but more about *that* later.

Intuitive people who see chakras with discolorations are witnessing the chakras' difficulties. So, for example, if we expected your root chakra to be red and instead it is a muddy brown, it could indicate a physical or emotional problem in this area. If you practice, you'll be able to see some colors on different parts of people's bodies. You would not want to diagnose people with the information that you receive, but it's helpful in learning where the seat of the problem may originate. Remember that this is not a literal system, but a perceptual system and the more you practice, the better you will be at determining when something is amiss.

Let's go through the chakras, from first to seventh, explaining what they traditionally represent. But don't take it all too literally because it's a representational system.

The First Chakra: The Root

The first chakra is at the base of your spine. It is your root chakra, often associated with the color red. This chakra connects you to the earth and all of the earth's energy, often called "Mother Earth" energy. This chakra flows vertically. The only other chakra that flows vertically is the crown chakra at the top of your head. The other chakras flow through your body from front to back.

The root chakra is very important. It is the source of our grounding to the earth and holds us in our place in the world. If we are ungrounded, we are in fact untethered, like an untied balloon that is floating around.

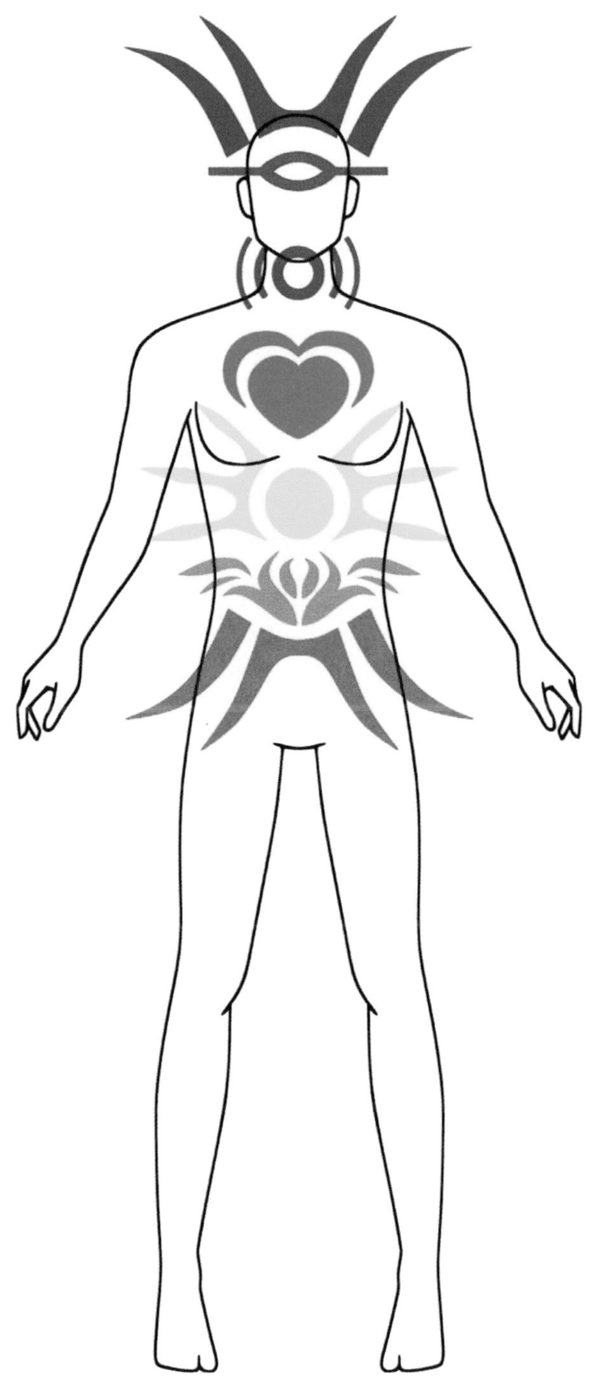

THE CHAKRAS

Lack of grounding manifests in many emotional and physical ways. A typical experience of being ungrounded is a feeling of separation from others, that you are "at sixes and sevens," at a loss for a comfortable place to settle in your life—or in other words, rootless. We all know of someone in our life who we consider "spacey." They float around from idea to idea, from relationship to relationship. They change jobs frequently, and in general, don't seem to be able to stick with anything.

If we are ungrounded, we are in fact untethered, like an untied balloon that is floating around.

Being ungrounded doesn't allow you to think clearly from a base of rootedness. You are energetically homeless. You may have a feeling of dissociation, of being out of your body. Those experiences can be great! I'm all for astral travel. However, it should be done consciously. People who are ungrounded aren't consciously deciding to take a little ride on a winged horse and float off into another dimension. They are simply unable to stay in their bodies.

In order to understand the experience of being ungrounded, you could try remembering a time when you were very ill and ran a high fever. Fever tends to unground us from our body and creates a feeling of rootlessness. Remember the feeling that you had when you were very sick and you felt as if you were floating? That is the feeling of being rootless, of not being connected to the earth and grounded. Of course, it occurs to greater and lesser extents and being sick with a high fever is an extreme experience.

People who feel dissociated (detached from immediate surroundings or even from physical and emotional experience) often feel like this for long periods of time and find it quite distressing. When I worked at a mental hospital as a young therapist (never a terrific idea if you're an empath and a psychic), many people were severely ungrounded. I would not have given it that label then, but I know now that they had absolutely no connection to the earth and to reality. They were floating around somewhere and could not bring themselves down to earth, a very difficult experience for them. Many people did not even remember what it felt like to be grounded or rooted in the earth. One of the things I liked to do with these patients was to take them outside and have them lie down on the grass. Sometimes just the feeling of the earth beneath them provided the comfort of being grounded. I am not saying that mental illness or severe dissociation can be cured by lying on the grass. But if you feel that you are ungrounded, as if you are separate and apart or floating above your body, it's a good exercise to lie down on the ground and feel its gravitational pull drawing you closer to Mother Earth.

In my current energy work, when someone is not grounded energetically, it looks to me as though an x-ray or negative is being pulled out of the top of their head, like a shadow of them exiting their body. Some people are very pulled out, even as far as their waist. Being pulled out of your body or being ungrounded can be very dangerous. In addition to the possibility that you might walk into the street when a car is coming or cut yourself chopping vegetables, being ungrounded can have serious effects on relationships. Likewise, if you're unable to remember to get to appointments or unable to be at your work on time, you can lose your financial stability and your friends.

It is impossible to be grounded all the time. We all leave our bodies if things become too difficult emotionally, sometimes even if they become too difficult physically. Be aware and watch for this in yourself. Remember that grounding exercises, like meditation, can help you stay present in your body.

GROUNDING

We often forget how important it is to ground ourselves on a regular basis. We may live in office buildings, sometimes many floors above the earth itself. We need to remember we are connected to, and part of, the earth. Too many people rarely touch the ground. They go from an apartment several stories up to an office building several stories up, never really feeling the earth except when transitioning in a subway, bus or car. This pattern can be very disturbing to your energy and your physical and mental health. Grounding exercises, though simple, are very important.

ONE

Walk to your backyard, a park, or similar space, planting your feet firmly on the Earth as you go.

Take your shoes off, lie down on the ground, and feel a connection to the Earth. Take some slow, deep breaths and allow yourself to feel the "heartbeat" of Earth.

Notice gravity. Notice growing things pushing up from the Earth and down into her. Notice the weight of your hands and your feet, your arms and your legs and your head.

TWO

Walk on the grass and on the beach in your bare feet. The waves are like Earth's heartbeat—rhythmic.

Feel the rhythm and the pace of the Earth beneath your feet. Know that you are connected to Earth.

The Second Chakra: Life Force

The second chakra is below your navel, and is associated with the color orange. This area is where our life force resides because this chakra is all about creation and energy. Artists and actors and those who are very conscious of their performance and presence in the world have a strong second chakra. People who are ill or feel very weak or tired will have a correspondingly weaker second chakra. If you have a second chakra imbalance, it may represent sexual issues as well.

A gentleman came into my office with many second chakra issues. He was always tired, always grumpy, and was having sexual performance issues. We talked about these problems and how they are influencing his life. It became pretty clear to me that he had a lot of blockage in and around the second chakra. One sure sign of your second chakra being weak is that feeling of constant exhaustion; he was plagued by this problem. It was no wonder that he was having sexual problems as well. He was too tired. I did some energy work on him around these issues and around releasing blockages in that area. He immediately noticed after our sessions that his energy improved.

It's interesting that we are a society very focused on sexual functioning and how well someone performs in this area. Unblocking the second chakra and having it open and free not only releases our potential for accomplishing things, but the life force can also free us up in a sexual manner.

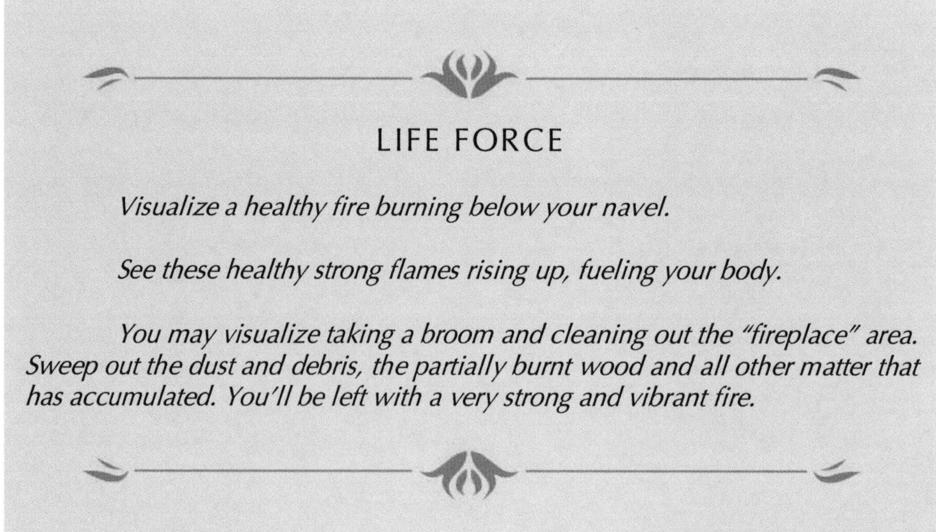

LIFE FORCE

Visualize a healthy fire burning below your navel.

See these healthy strong flames rising up, fueling your body.

You may visualize taking a broom and cleaning out the "fireplace" area. Sweep out the dust and debris, the partially burnt wood and all other matter that has accumulated. You'll be left with a very strong and vibrant fire.

The Third Chakra: The Solar Plexus

The third chakra is below your rib cage. This is the solar plexus and is associated with the Sun and the color yellow. The Sun is the source of light and allows not only plants and animals but people to grow. The diaphragm, a large, cup-shaped muscle that goes from your back to your front and separates the top of your body from the bottom of your body, is located in this area. Also associated with this chakra are the large intestine, stomach, pancreas, spleen, liver and gall bladder. Ungrounded people who "pull out of their body" or become seriously dissociated often are separated at the point of the solar plexus.

To me, this chakra represents the way that we feel we are perceived by others in the world. It's not our actual perception in the world, but our belief, our construct about how we think others see us. This is an important distinction. People with problems in this chakra area may often have difficulty in social situations, feel insecure, shy or very sensitive to insult and slight.

The wonderful thing about the third chakra is that it is where the Sun shines in. It is where we receive all of the beautiful energy from everyone around us. When it is in balance, we receive that information about how we are regarded and that makes us feel great.

It's very important to cultivate your own self-worth and then project it so others will perceive you in the way that you desire.

We have to be careful about our solar plexus. Suppose you are in a working environment and you feel that you are distrusted or perceived as "less than." This perception will affect the way that you do your work, the attitude you come to work with each day, how you talk to your boss, and how you process experiences, *even though it may not be the truth.*

Here's an amusing example about how we are perceived. I walk around in the world thinking that I'm five feet six inches tall. In reality, I'm exactly five feet tall. I project an image to people that's taller. I absolutely see myself as five feet six! As a result, when they find out how tall I am, people often say, "Gee, you really look taller." I actually project this from my solar plexus. I feel I'm taller, I pretend I'm taller, I think that people perceive me as taller, and so it happens. Throughout his whole life, my younger brother told me that he was five feet seven. I believed him. One day, he was standing next to his wife who's actually five feet four and they were the same height. I said to him, "You say you are five feet seven. Your wife is five feet four. You are both the same height. How is that possible?" He laughed and said, "Well I've been telling people I'm five feet seven and they believed me, so you believe me too." To which I replied, "Yes, but I've known you all your life." "Well, see? It worked," he answered. He also believed that he would be perceived as taller, and that's what happened.

In order to be successful in the world, it is very important that our solar plexus be in balance with our other energy. People notice the way that we feel about ourselves, and the way that we feel we are perceived may not be accurate at all. This is just one example of how important it is to have a balanced third chakra.

Great leaders and people who are good communicators often have a very strong third chakra. They know how they are perceived in the world in a way that is very powerful. It's very important to cultivate your own self-worth and then project it so others will perceive you in the way that you desire. Suppose, for example, that you will be speaking at an important meeting and you are nervous about the content and the reception you will get. Focusing on your third chakra before you have to speak, as in the exercise below, may prove valuable.

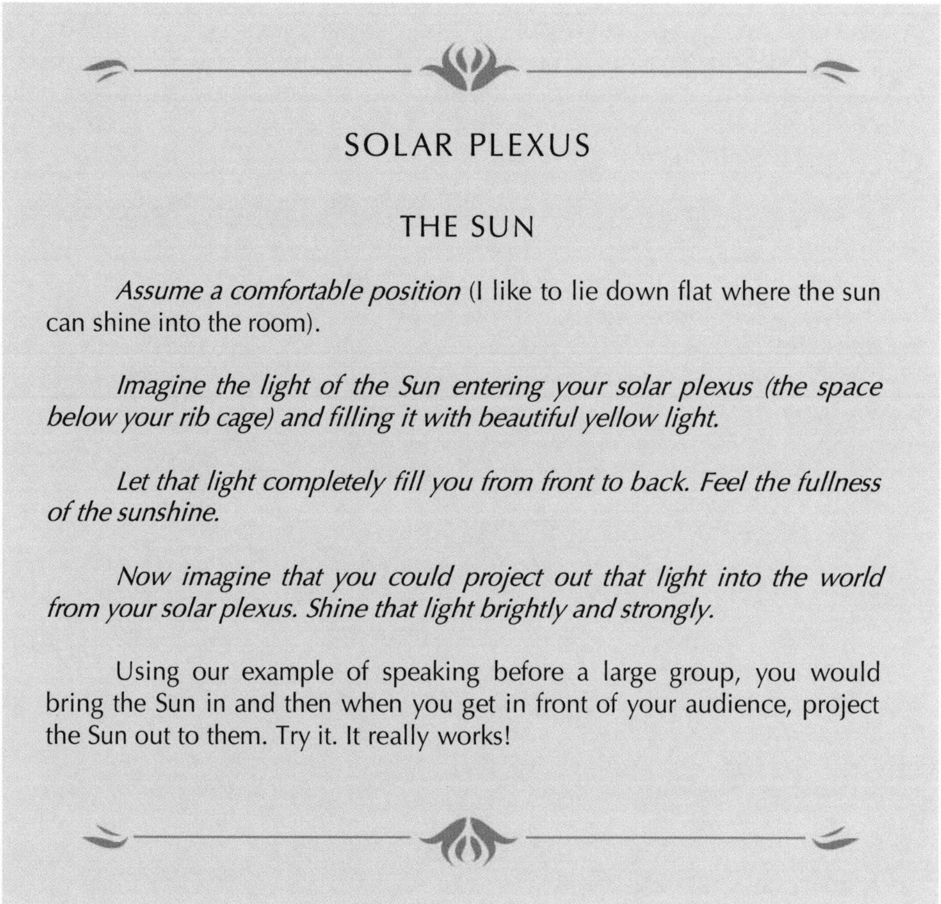

SOLAR PLEXUS

THE SUN

Assume a comfortable position (I like to lie down flat where the sun can shine into the room).

Imagine the light of the Sun entering your solar plexus (the space below your rib cage) and filling it with beautiful yellow light.

Let that light completely fill you from front to back. Feel the fullness of the sunshine.

Now imagine that you could project out that light into the world from your solar plexus. Shine that light brightly and strongly.

Using our example of speaking before a large group, you would bring the Sun in and then when you get in front of your audience, project the Sun out to them. Try it. It really works!

If you have breathing problems, it may be another indication that there are issues with the solar plexus. A second exercise to do in order to strengthen the solar plexus is a breathing exercise, a *pranayama*. *Prana* means "life force" in Sanskrit, *yama* means "control," and many breathing exercises are used in yogic practice. The following is used for meditation and also strengthens your breathing.

SOLAR PLEXUS BREATHING

Assume a comfortable position, either sitting or lying down. (When using this breath to meditate, one should not lie down, but for the purposes of this exercise, it may help to feel your belly moving up and down.)

Breathe in to the count of 4 through your nose, and out to the count of 8 through your mouth. (If you're gasping for breath, back that down to 2 and 4.)

Imagine that you can fill up your belly each time you take a breath. You may rest your hands on your belly to feel it expand and deflate. (If you've seen a small infant breathing, that's what inhalation and exhalation should look like: belly out with the in-*breath, and belly flat with the out-breath.)*

Try to work yourself up to longer combinations of breath, but never go to a point where you are gasping.

You will eventually be able to get your breath quite far. I have gotten myself up to 32/64 when doing meditation. That's a high number, but it is possible there are meditators who can accomplish even higher numbers.

The Fourth Chakra: The Heart

The fourth chakra is the heart chakra. It's associated with the color green and also the color rose. The heart chakra includes the area from your clavicle (collarbone) to your diaphragm; your whole rib cage area is included. Our deep feelings reside here. When we talk about our heart breaking or our heart being full, we are quite literally talking about the state of this chakra. But don't be confused. The heart chakra does not only include the heart, but the lungs and that whole area of the body as well. I think of this chakra in my visualizations as if it is divided by a vertical line down the middle, the left side representing the heart and the right side representing the lungs. Therefore, heart issues such as love, hatred, compassion, belonging and rejection are associated with the left side of the chakra, and issues related to the lungs, such as grief or deep sadness, with the right side.

We may be struggling with difficulty in any part of our body, but ultimately it is the ceasing of the beating of the heart that is deemed the end of our life. I have a client who is a coroner, and one of the things she often says to me is "everyone dies because their heart stops." True, that is literally the death of the physical body, when the heart stops. Obviously, we need this chakra to be working well and in tune with the world in order to survive. Therefore, the well-being of this chakra is very important, not only to be alive but to be emotionally healthy. This means, of course, cardiovascular exercise, but it also means being kind and good to yourself. So whether you think of the heart as a muscle, or you think of the heart as a chakra, it represents the seat of your emotions, so tend to it well.

HEART CHAKRA

Get into a comfortable position in a quiet room. (If it is not possible to have total quiet, put on noise-canceling headphones or ear plugs.)

Listen to the sound of your heart beating. Is it slow? Is it rapid? Is it even or does the pace change? We can answer a lot of questions about how we are feeling by listening to the beating of our heart.

Now listen to the beating of your heart in the extremities of your body: feel your pulse in your legs or ankles, your arms, your throat. Gently put your hand on your neck and feel the pulse. Feel the essence of the blood flowing through your body.

Picture your physical heart. See the blood flowing through, pumping with each beat, with each "lub-dub."

Imagine yourself entering your heart, walking through the chambers and watching how perfectly each beat is synchronized and how beautifully this organ works, from the moment of birth to the moment of death, almost flawlessly.

Send gratitude to your heart for the hard work that it does every day. This organ the size of your fist literally oxygenates your body, pushing the blood everywhere that it needs to go. Sit with gratitude for a few moments and allow yourself to calm.

Now put your hand on your chest and feel your heart beat. It probably has slowed to a more even rhythm. Enjoy.

The Fifth Chakra: The Throat

The fifth chakra is the throat chakra, associated with the color blue, the blue of the sky. This chakra is the source of your voice, the way that you verbally communicate. It spans from your jaw down to your clavicle area. If your speech is stifled or restricted, you could have issues with this chakra. Throat chakra issues are commonplace in our society. I'll step out of being politically correct here and say that I rarely meet a woman who does not have some throat chakra issues. I think it's often more difficult for women to speak up about their feelings, which is not to say that men never have issues in this area. The stifling of one's voice often means there may be problems in the throat chakra.

Many people who have been repressed during their life have fifth chakra issues. They are unable to voice their feelings and have problems communicating effectively with others. They also have difficulty standing up for themselves. If you have no voice, you have no power or strength to communicate. Those of us who have been told to shut up, be quiet, or made to feel that our opinions don't matter, often have throat chakra issues. Try to pay attention when you get a sore throat. Often I seem to get a sore throat when I have repressed some emotions that I didn't communicate to someone in a way that I needed to.

THROAT CHAKRA

With your mind's eye, enter your throat area.

Feel if places are tight or restricted. Sometimes it helps to gently rest your hands on your throat. Notice if that makes you feel restricted or in some way tight.

Stretch your jaw, opening your mouth as wide as possible. Feel if there is pulling or lack of motion or difficulty doing so. Never push yourself to a situation of pain, just do a gentle stretch.

Notice the area from the top of your neck to where it meets your body, including the place where muscles attach at the back of your head. Send light and energy to these spaces, allowing them to relax, allowing your shoulders to lower.

Because this chakra involves our ability to communicate, it is important to be gentle when working in this area.

Throat chakra issues can also manifest as issues with the jaw, ear, and neck. When I worked as an intern many years ago at a veterans' hospital, the doctor who was training us made a funny comment about the neck. He said that we ask this very slim stalk to hold up something about the weight of a bowling ball. Now, we're referring to a New York "ten pin" bowling ball, a big heavy ball between twelve and sixteen pounds. So when your neck hurts, remember that it's doing a very big job holding up this large heavy object. Be kind to your neck and your throat chakra.

The Sixth Chakra: The Third Eye

The sixth chakra is located in the space between your eyebrows, known as the "third eye." It is associated with the color indigo. This chakra governs things that we know without seeing, our vision that is not the vision of our eyes, but our inner "knowing."

The third eye is often the trickiest chakra to talk about. What does it look like? Do we all have a funny little eye in the middle of our head like some of those Hindu statues? Is our third eye always open? Do some of us have it stuck closed? Well, like any other chakra it can either be working well or not.

When I do a body scan to assess someone's health, I always close my eyes. I wasn't aware of this until about a year ago when someone said, "You can see me when your eyes are closed?" I said, "I didn't know I close my eyes." Yet I did each time I wanted to "look." I close my eyes in order to allow my third eye to be the most open. I found that in order to see with this chakra I need to limit the stimuli that come from my other eyes. From a scientific perspective, when we close our eyes, we activate the part of our nervous system that relaxes us and our awareness is turned inward.

I believe the third eye developed for several reasons, but one of them is to protect us from physical harm and danger. Listen to those voices if you get something telling you, *Don't drive home that way, take the other route.* There is probably a reason. That's your third eye doing its job. From a purely pragmatic point of view, this sixth sense is the sense that keeps us out of harm's way. Of course, it's been used for much loftier and more complicated purposes, but I believe that's where it began.

Whenever people doubt that they have a third eye, I always give them this little example. It makes me laugh. I ask them, "Would you like me to prove to you that you have a third eye and that you can sense things beyond your usual five senses?" Most people say yes, and I say, "Okay, here goes: you're driving down the highway in a car and all of a sudden you feel as if someone's looking at you. You turn around and there's a truck driver looking straight down at you. You can literally feel him looking at you. How could we possibly feel that if we didn't have another sense?" We are in a closed metal box going sixty miles an hour and we feel someone's eyes on us. We feel they are looking at us.

Truck drivers have an amazing sense in this regard. We know that they sense our presence as well. One of the little games that I sometimes play when I'm bored on the highway (and I'm often bored when I'm driving) is to send my energy while looking at truck drivers and wait for them to turn and acknowledge me. Be careful playing this game that you don't drive off the road, but you can see how the fact that you are concentrating on them actually brings their attention toward you. There's no other explanation for this phenomenon, other than that we have additional abilities beyond our five senses.

Most people don't pay attention to the third eye and don't use it. It's a lot like learning how to play baseball when you're a kid and then not playing again for twenty years. You don't expect that you're going to be the best pitcher, catcher or runner after all those years, do you? The same is true of the third eye. We may have effectively used it when we were small children, and been told by our families not to pay attention to our imaginary friends or things that we "knew." Our culture does not really create an atmosphere to develop third eye skills. So you can be a little rusty when you try to open it up again, but everything in this life that's worth doing requires practice and persistence. So aside from the driving experiment, how can you practice using your third eye? You might try the following exercises.

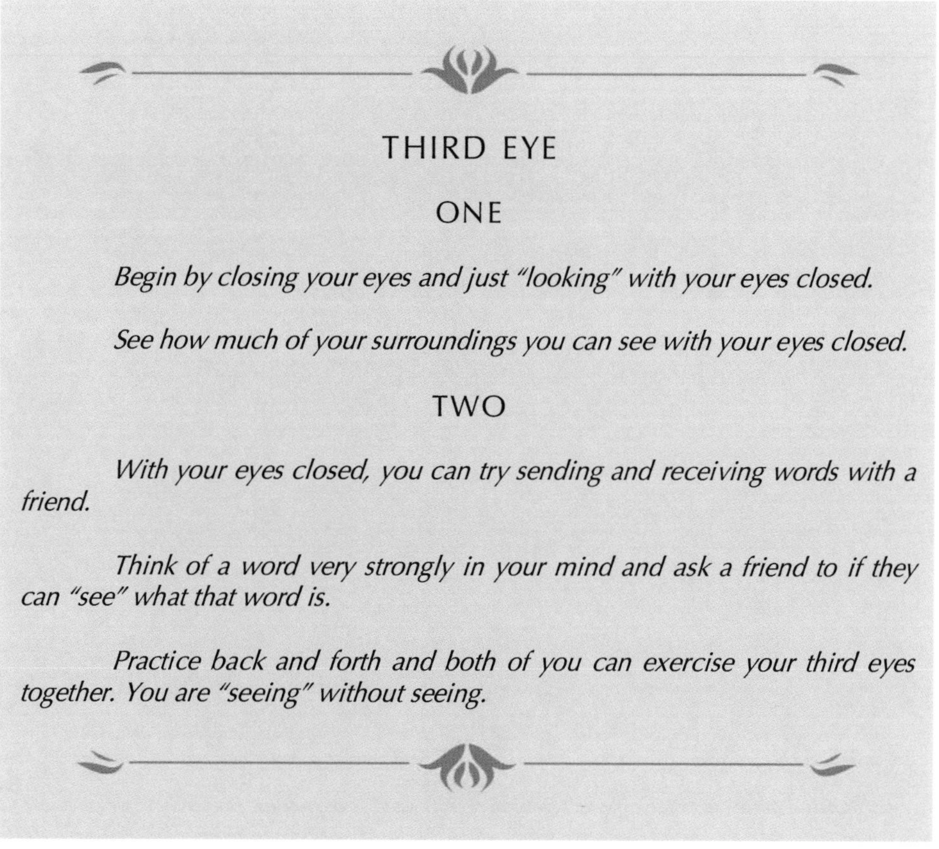

THIRD EYE

ONE

Begin by closing your eyes and just "looking" with your eyes closed.

See how much of your surroundings you can see with your eyes closed.

TWO

With your eyes closed, you can try sending and receiving words with a friend.

Think of a word very strongly in your mind and ask a friend to if they can "see" what that word is.

Practice back and forth and both of you can exercise your third eyes together. You are "seeing" without seeing.

The Seventh Chakra: The Crown

The seventh chakra is the crown chakra, our connection to the Divine. Whether you call it the collective unconscious, God, the Universal Light, or just the Source of All, this chakra is that connection. It is associated with the color violet. Remember that this is a vertical chakra, flowing up and down.

This chakra is the place from which we channel wisdom and receive information that is not our knowing, but is from God. It is where our best self truly comes from. The more we can open our crown chakra, the more we can receive divine Light, and the more Light we can give to the world. We allow the God light into our soul.

When people speak of hearing voices, they are talking about hearing them through their crown chakra. When people channel individuals, either people who have passed or guides, they are channeling them by allowing their crown chakra to be very open. Sometimes I think that the most able channelers are people who are best able to open their crown chakra. When fully open, it's about the size of a half dollar. This opening is a good thing; bad things will not come in. When you are in your sacred space or other safe place, practice visualizing the opening up of your crown chakra.

CROWN CHAKRA

Remember that the crown chakra is vertical; it goes up and down. My personal image is something like the Hubble telescope, which opens up its big lens so that the light of the stars can enter.

ONE

The crown chakra, when closed, can be almost the size of a pinhead, and when open, can be the size of a half dollar. Practice imagining that you can open the center of the top of your head to the size of a half dollar.

TWO

Visualize your crown chakra at the top of your head opening up to receive all that is Divine. You will be surprised what comes in: love and light, hope and happiness, joy.

See the white light that comes in through your crown, and whatever information or wisdom that you can receive at this moment. Allow it to enter. Be patient. Sometimes it takes a while to happen.

In order to allow it to happen more easily, visualize all of the knowledge and all of the information and all of the things that are known in the world.

Ask for a specific thing to come into your knowing. It can be any detail that you wish to know, or just a general feeling that you would like to understand. You will be surprised and amazed that you will often get answers to questions.

Remember, when you are done with this exercise, it is good to return your crown chakra to the slightly open position. It is important with all of your chakras that you return them to the slightly open position when you are done with any of the exercises.

CHAPTER FOUR

Guides: Teachers Within and Without

Whether you follow a mainstream religion or choose a more individualized path, you do not have to travel on your spiritual journey alone; nor, in fact, should you. You will learn and grow safely and optimally with a teacher. Gurus, ministers, shamans, rabbis and others are, of course, present to offer instruction and counsel as fellow humans who have trained and traveled on their own spiritual journeys. Other mentors may be those trained in spiritual direction who, like therapists, engage in a conversation with the soul to help you answer your own questions of faith. And, there are countless teachers from many different disciplines offering workshops, retreats and classes that you may benefit from greatly.

In this chapter, we will discuss how to find a spiritual teacher, but first I would like to introduce you to the teachers you will find within who are waiting to share their wisdom and support and who may already be known to you: your spirit guides.

Spirit Guides

As our aides and companions on the path, spirit guides are so prevalent in all our work that it is worthwhile inviting them into your life as soon as you feel ready. Beautiful angels and saints are perhaps the best known and most universal of spirit guides, but there are countless other personifications: animals, people, even trees. Some will arrive in dreams, some in guided meditation, sometimes they just come. It really doesn't matter how your spirit guides manifest; all gates to the city and all spirit guides lead to your higher self. They are put in your consciousness to help you, are always benevolent and can be called upon whenever you need them. Spirit guides can be thought of in many ways. To me, they have always been intermediaries of the Divine Consciousness. I believe that they are assigned to us to help us on our way. We just have to create a space for them.

It doesn't matter what you call your spirit guides. In many cultures, what we would call spirit guides others call ancestors, actual forbears who come to help in times of need. When I was a little girl, many of my Catholic friends would collect saint cards at mass. We can consider these cards as a type of spirit guide, chosen for the saint's particular skill or area of expertise. For example, St. Christopher, the patron saint of travelers, was chosen when you were planning a long trip; St. Jude (a personal favorite), was the patron saint of lost causes and so on. They served the purpose of helping with a difficult time or fearful passage, much as Native American animal spirit guides are chosen for the qualities of the animal they represent: a bear for strength, an owl for wisdom, etc. In taking on these totemic animals as spirit guides, we hope to gain from their particular skills and use them to help us in a guided meditation. In Hindu belief structure, there are thousands of Gods and Goddesses and people choose one that they most closely identify with in terms of personality and life goals. Often, the person is even named for that God or Goddess. The universal concept of spirit guides exists in all belief structures. We have just broadened their context to include those of all cultures so that we may create our own belief system that works for us.

Spirit guides are put in your consciousness to help you and can be called upon whenever you need them.

When I was young girl, in fact, for as long as I can remember, I had a spirit guide, although I didn't know that's what she was at the time. She was very tall, taller than a human could possibly be, with long silver hair down to her knees. She wore a long, iridescent silver dress and seemed to have silver skin and even silver eyes. Whenever I was upset, sad or lonely she would come to me. I would place my head on her lap and she would stroke my hair. She is still with me. She comes in times of trouble and sadness. She never speaks to me, but calms and comforts me. I expect she will be with me for my whole life. I don't know if she represents a human, an alien or an angel. I just know that she has always been with me. I had no words to describe her function until I was much older. I just knew she would always be there when I needed her.

Angels have become so stereotyped and commercialized that I almost think of them as dashboard accessories, but they are prevalent in some form in many religions and individual practices. The way that I was trained, spirit guides are animals, but I don't see any reason why they can't be angels, saints or just people in your life who have passed over who may have given you guidance. They might return to help you on your journey. One reason why shamanic training was a good discipline for me was because I did not want to choose a specific deity as a guide. I wanted many spirit guides for many different purposes.

Spirit guides tend to change over time, depending on our state of mind and the issues we need to work on. Be aware, however, that just as there is evil, there are dark spirits. It is pretty easy to tell who your spirit guides are and who might be working in a negative way. Spirit guides will never ask you to do anything that goes against your basic nature or your conscience. They will always give you advice in harmony with your way of thinking. They will bring new ideas and unique ways of solving problems. I encourage you to look for them everywhere.

The Personal Totem Pole

Now that we know there are guides to help us on the spiritual path and are aware of our energy centers, the chakras, I would like to introduce you to a process called the personal totem pole, wherein each chakra is represented by a spirit guide animal. It can be a good place for you to start thinking about guides and what each individual animal's spirit represents. Your animal guides will tell you things you need to know about yourself on a deeper level and will often take you on journeys. Part of my own spiritual training was based on this process. Originated by E. S. Gallegos in the 1980s, the Personal Totem Pole Process© is an accessible yet powerful method of inner exploration. I am taking some liberties to simplify the material and offer it as a starting point for your own exploration. I would encourage anyone interested to seek out some of the beautifully written material on this type of deep imagery. [1]

The personal totem pole is used in conjunction with a meditation practice that allows for spiritual "journeying." (We will talk more about guided meditation in Chapter Ten.) There are many methods of journeying, but I will give you an idea of where to start. This method can be understood on several levels. It can be understood on the psychological level, integrating different parts of your personality by going through the chakras and inviting an animal into each one, ultimately integrating them all. Or, you could just see the process as giving yourself a sense of well-being by recognizing all the different voices that speak within you, and where they speak from. This ritual way of looking at the concept is quite fun, and shows us that we have guides who help us to achieve the goals on our path.

Totem Examples

Taking the third eye as an example, many people have birds as spirit guides for this chakra totem. When you think about the third eye, this approach makes sense. Birds can fly way ahead of us and see what's before us and report back what is in our future. They are not tethered to the ground, but can travel to distant places and return with important information.

In terms of your totem pole, the throat chakra is another interesting place to look. As we saw earlier, this area is often a place where people have issues about their true voice. If our voice is strong and clear in the world, we might see a vital and strong animal. If we are feeling unheard, we might find an animal that does not have a voice. I often learn that people have rabbits for their throat chakra

---

[1] Gallegos, Eligio Stephen. The Personal Totem Pole: Animal Imagery, the Chakras, and Psychotherapy. Moon Bear Press.

guide. Rabbits are, of course, voiceless. They are also prey animals. Therefore, we may understand that our throat chakra is probably about the things that we aren't saying and from which we may be running away. Having this animal as a guide can help you to become strong in your communication as you realize that your throat chakra needs strengthening.

In your totem pole you may have any animal for any chakra, but let's just draw a theoretical one here.

PERSONAL TOTEM POLE

TOTEM POLE

MEETING A SPIRIT GUIDE

Close your eyes. Take some slow, deep breaths to relax.

Visualize a chakra. See what animal comes to mind.

Think about what that animal's characteristics are and see what those traits could mean about the present state of your being.

DRAWING YOUR TOTEM POLE

Visualize each chakra one by one. As you stay in your consciousness with that chakra, ask that an animal guide come forth. Introduce yourself.

Ask this spirit guide to introduce itself and ask why it has come. It may have come to solve a specific problem for you, or to help with a specific need.

Try to hear what it has to say. It is often very useful information.

Continue by meditating on each of your chakras and see what animal comes to you. Don't over-think this step, just let it happen. Over time, you can change what animal represents a chakra as you change and grow.

Make a drawing with all of the animals in their chakras and then look at your totem pole and think about what each animal might mean to you. For example, if you see a bear in one of your chakras, it could mean that you feel strong and vital, but it might also mean that you feel angry. The animals' aspect and condition will give you further insight into the condition of each chakra.

Think carefully about what it says about you that you have matched a particular chakra with a particular animal. In this way, you can learn a lot about yourself.

It's a good idea to date this totem pole and continue to draw new ones each year. It's very interesting to see how you evolve and change and which animals or representatives you choose.

Once you have created your totem pole, you will have a set of spirit guides, a sort of Council of Elders that you can call together to make significant decisions in your life. I really enjoy my Council of Elders and call them often. I bring them around the fire and ask each of them to speak for a different aspect of my being so that I can make the best decision for my own highest and best good and the highest and best good of my service to the Light.

Remember that guides may change or several guides may appear. I myself have had several animals representing my heart chakra alone over the years. Try to be patient and listen to what they have to say and where they take you. Often, where they take you is a metaphor for an experience in your life as you know it now.

Enjoy their beauty, wisdom and guidance. They will always be there for you.

Choosing a Spiritual Teacher

Something strange I have often observed about people is that they will research which television set or breed of dog they should buy months before making a decision, but when it comes to choices about people, their decisions are often quick and less thought through. I am certainly not telling you that your gut instinct is not important. It is key and can be tuned to help in every aspect of your life, especially the spiritual. However, there are important criteria regarding who to trust about spiritual guidance and some "rules of the road" are probably in order.

One note before we address the dos and don'ts. Because in the spiritual realm we often deal with people who walk between two worlds, be aware that some can be a bit flaky.

For example, I was once going to a Native American ceremony led by my spiritual teacher. He gave me driving directions and said it should take me about forty-five minutes from my home. This was before I had a GPS. I thought that his directional guidance would be as wonderful as his spiritual guidance. But after three hours of wandering through wooded areas, I pulled into a fire station and got some help. When I finally arrived, pretty much at the end of the ceremony, a woman said to me, "You took outer directions from Richard?"

I trust Richard, my teacher, with my soul, but I know now I would not trust him with telling me how to get from here to the corner! That is probably because he has the kind of brain that doesn't focus on these kinds of issues; they're not important to him. That, by anyone's standards, probably qualifies as flaky. But his flakiness has nothing to do with the important teachings that have guided my spiritual life. Making a determination about someone's reliability in a spiritual area is often different from their outer reliability about things such as driving directions.

Some Warning Signs

We all think we'd know it if we are being abused but there are some subtle hints that should not be overlooked. If a spiritual teacher asks you to do something that is uncomfortable to you in any way, either physically or emotionally, that should be a warning sign. Let's talk about some warning signs to watch out for.

First, anyone who asks you for money beyond an hourly fee for their services should be looked at with some caution. Unfortunately, there are a lot of unscrupulous people and institutions out there and we are all vulnerable when it comes to caring for our own heart and soul. If someone is asking you to contribute or donate money or other assets, beware. I'm not talking about entrance fees or course tuition; I'm talking about donations of any significance. I charge for my time. I will see people without cost sometimes, but I normally charge for my time.

Whether it is an exchange of money for services, a barter agreement or other arrangement, there's an important concept called an "energy exchange." That energy exchange is a contract that you make with someone when you give them something and they give you something in return. That exchange should be reasonable and fair and the area of spiritual birth and creation is no exception. I'm not talking about classic "passing the plate" at church. That practice has been accepted ritual for a long time. It is also, at least in theory, anonymous.

Any organization that uses shaming and blaming is not a place you should be.

If someone asks you to wear specific clothing or something that feels like a uniform, you should be concerned. Certainly, if you're entering a monastery you should be dressed in appropriate robes. But if you are asked to wear a uniform of some sort all the time, that is something that may indicate possible coercion. Wearing white on a holiday or being asked to take off your shoes seems quite within the range of normal to me. (In fact, I require everyone who enters my office to take off their shoes, unless they have an orthopedic issue.) If you are required to purchase objects of worship, that's similar to being asked to wear a uniform. If you are asked to buy meditation bells, that's a minor thing. But if it is something expensive, you should be hearing another kind of bell.

Another danger sign is being asked to recruit others. It is not your job as a student to bring in other students; that can be a sign of a cult. Bringing in members and revenue should be the responsibility of the people who run the organization, not its students. Again, use your judgment. I recently spent several hours standing in front of a supermarket to recruit new members from my women's chorus. That's not the kind of thing I'm talking about. If you are made to feel responsible for bringing in members, or if it is required, those things should concern you.

If you are made to feel inadequate in any way or embarrassed, that's a bad sign. Any organization that uses shaming and blaming is not a place you should be. Any individual who makes you feel "less than" in any way is also not a good teacher for you. There are enough places in life that make us feel bad. Being a student on a spiritual path, while challenging at times, should be a positive experience.

Finding the Positives

I have talked about a lot of no's. What are the yes's when looking for a teacher? First, it's good to have someone who has some training. Whether that person is your rabbi or your priest or a shamanic teacher, training is crucial. It is never wrong to ask someone about his or her background and ideally that information should be available in their public profile, with dates. To know where someone has been is significant in order to get a sense of whether it's where you want to be going. It is not necessary that someone have formal spiritual training; many of us have backgrounds in other areas such as helping professions of all sorts. But most of us have "interned" under another teacher. Check out their teacher. Some individuals have had many different spiritual teachers. Look into this as well.

You want a teacher who has taken the time to do his or her own spiritual exploration, either in a formal or individual setting. Learn what their ideas, method and philosophy are before you trust yourself to them. If they have written articles or a book, read those materials and see if they resonate with you. Ideally, you will feel safe and excited. It's also not inappropriate to ask for references. Privacy issues could make this a bit delicate, but it's worth asking.

Take a test drive. I do a free fifteen-minute chat with people if they request it. I also tell everyone I work with that this is a match, a relationship and you should be confident it is a good relationship before you commit. I tell people that the first session is to see if we are a good match, and that I will not be offended if we are not. I will even suggest other teachers who might be a better fit.

CHAPTER FIVE

Ways to be Psychic

If you are new to the concept of intuitive knowledge, I think it's worthwhile to explain some of the different ways that people can be psychic. I'm sure you've wondered if you have these abilities and want to know what they mean. Just as there are many ways you may receive tangible gifts, you can be given spiritual gifts as well. Most of us have some ability. I believe that they are hard wired in the brain, but like a muscle, can be exercised and developed. You can increase that ability no matter how much you have, and become better at seeing and knowing things in a psychic manner.

Because our culture is an evidence- and science-based one, it's often difficult for sensitive and intuitive people to acknowledge their own psychic abilities. Even harder is the ridicule and denial they may face if they share these experiences. It is especially important for parents to be aware of their child's abilities, *all* of them, so that they will feel safe, respected and understood. They should be given an opportunity to develop these gifts, which have the potential to help them and humanity in extraordinary ways. I would like to take a moment to share some thoughts about this topic.

Advice for Parents

Be aware of the gifts that your child might have and seek out someone who can help them learn to live with and use their gifts. If you have a child who is experiencing social discomfort as I was, it's important to find someone who understands this kind of experience and who can contextualize and normalize it for them. If their perceptions are denied, these children can become damaged. Imagine what it would be like to see something and have people tell you it's not there. The two choices are: you're crazy, or the other people are crazy. That's not an easy situation for a child to be in.

When you are an empath, for example, not only can you feel the people that you are close to, but you can "plug in" to just about anybody. You feel their pain, their happiness and sadness, basically everything as you would feel it yourself. It can be exhausting to feel what others feel all the time and it can be confusing to try to understand where you begin and someone else ends. It's a particularly difficult challenge in social and romantic situations.

Empaths, if not helped when they are children, will often grow up having emotional problems. They will remain confused about the boundary between themselves and other people. They will sense and feel things that sometimes frighten people. It is very important for an empath to get some help; not the kind of help that says "You need a psychiatric assessment," but the kind of help that says "You need a teacher who can help you learn how to use this very special skill."

I am in no way implying that there aren't children who might present with some of the above behavior or who have other issues that might indeed be psychologically or physiologically based. Of course, these children will need proper evaluation.

How do we treat our children when they tell us that they hear voices or when they speak to an "imaginary friend?" Genuinely psychic people (which means all of us to some degree) are vulnerable to the perceptions of others once they realize that the world is not made up of people who see, hear and feel what they do. You need to be aware that your child might have a gift, which may be especially true if there are psychics in the family: Aunt Gertrude who always knew who was calling on the phone, Uncle Robert who named the exact day when he would die or that spooky cousin of yours who would speak your words at the same time you did. You need to allow your children to understand that they have these special gifts and abilities.

Parents should be aware of their child's abilities so that they will feel safe, respected and understood.

I see a lot of these children in my practice. They are usually young teens who feel quite disturbed by feeling different from their peers. They feel as if they are strangers to the world. Unless their experiences are regarded as normal, they'll continue to be strangers and outsiders.

My own teenage years occurred during the "Age of Aquarius" period. Ouija boards and other similar things were big in those days. I had a ball suspended from the ceiling in my room, one of those little rubber balls that attaches to a little paddle. The ball and the stretchy rubber band had broken off the paddle, and I attached them to my ceiling with a stapler. I would enjoy making the ball sway by using my mind. (Don't get overly impressed; I can't bend a spoon. But I could move this ball and make it swing back and forth.)

When I was about twelve years old, I invited a bunch of friends for a sleepover party. In order to impress them, I told them how I could mentally move the ball. They thought I was kidding or that it would be some kind of trick. Well, I was pretty angry that they were laughing at me, so I really got that ball to swing back and forth, almost hitting the ceiling. Much to my surprise, all of the girls started screaming at the top of their lungs. My father came running in, hastily throwing on his robe over his underwear, shouting, "What's going on girls, does somebody need to go to the hospital?" In an utter cacophony, they all told him what had happened. He just looked at them with a disgusted expression and said, "You woke me up for *that* ?"

Again, I was very lucky that I lived in a family where psychic ability was considered normal. I tell the story in order to show you that it can be very difficult for a child to be accepted for who they are when they have psychic ability. Our awareness of it as parents and caregivers is necessary and can be damaging if ignored.

The Empath (Empathy)

An empath is someone who can not only sympathize with the emotions of people or animals (or for that matter, plants), but can also feel those same emotions as they occur. I'll give you an example. Anyone who has children has probably had the following experience. While making dinner with you, your child cuts himself with a knife. You can actually feel the pain of that knife entering your finger. You may even "see" the cut. It's a normal response that many people experience. But for an empath it's how she experiences the world all of the time.

One of the indicators that you might be an empath is that people frequently say to you, "Can you read my mind or something?" Being empathic is actually feeling what someone else feels. This occurrence usually happens in real time but can sometimes be triggered by a violent TV show or even a long distance vision.

Let me give you a funny example from my own life. As a responsible pet owner, when I got a kitten, I had her spayed. The day after her surgery, I noticed I was feeling abdominal pains and discomfort and a "pulling" feeling in my belly. It was a kind of "phantom" pain. I noticed that I felt it more when I was in certain places in my house. Suddenly, I realized that I was actually feeling the cat. I felt the surgical stitches and the discomfort and lethargy from her anesthesia as if it were happening to me.

Now, I have been doing this work for a long time, but it never occurred to me that I could feel animals as well. I am inordinately fond of this cat, so perhaps I am more connected to her than I might have been to other animals. She healed and I learned a valuable lesson: as empaths, we are especially connected to those we love, whether two- or four-legged beings.

Most people who are empaths have no idea that others don't feel the way that they do. When I was child, I didn't know there was any other way to be, in fact, I thought that other people could feel everything that the people around them felt. I thought that they were being colossally insensitive when they didn't realize that Susie was really sad or that Charles had a stomach ache. If you have some abilities, this kind of experience is probably true for you too. You grow up thinking that it's normal, and it is quite an awakening to realize that you see and feel differently. Sometimes I feel that others see in black and white while I see in color.

Empathy at Work

Many years ago when I was beginning my work as a therapist, one of my first assignments was in a mental hospital. It's not a good idea to put an empath in a mental hospital, especially an empath that doesn't yet know much about her skills. It was awfully "noisy" in my body and my mind. There was a lot of pain, and some people are very loud "broadcasters." It's clear what they are feeling both physically and emotionally.

I remember one young woman who kept claiming that she was suicidal and because she was, in fact, saying it every day, people stopped listening. Because I was very junior to just about everyone there, I reported this to my supervisor. He said, "Mary Jane will never kill herself; she talks about it too much" (actually a ridiculous assumption). One afternoon when I was talking to Mary Jane, I felt her intent so strongly that I actually felt as if I was suicidal. And I "saw" what she was going to do—her intended plan. She was going to take the drugs that she had squirreled away over a period of weeks and end her life. Luckily, I was able to convince an orderly to search her room. He found the drugs and removed them.

For quite some time after that incident I felt mostly anger from Mary Jane. And even though I had "heard" her broadcast her intention to die by her own hands and was able to stop it, this occurrence was not considered as wonderful as you would think by the hospital. Rather, it was regarded as more of an oddity. I think the staff thought that I was going to challenge them on their cases and step in with my assessments, when really I had just had a lucky shot. A lot of jockeying for position and approval was going on at the hospital and I think my actions were perceived as threatening. It was very difficult to continue my work and help the patients who I was there to help. In this case, being an empath was not the greatest asset.

While we are on the subject of mental illness, people frequently ask me about the relationship between mental illness and psychic ability. I have come to believe that one can be mentally ill and psychic or mentally ill and not at all psychic or psychic and not a bit mentally ill. Given the number of people that I've seen over the years, there doesn't appear to be a correlation. It's incredibly difficult when someone is mentally ill and psychic because it is hard to distinguish between delusions and visions. I often wonder if the visions might increase the odds of someone becoming mentally ill if that person is misunderstood and treated poorly by the people around them.

In the days since working at the mental hospital, I have trained rigorously to understand my empathic abilities and learn to use them to help others in an open way and with their full permission. When someone comes into my office in pain, I can "sample" that pain and feel it in my body. The same is true of emotions. This ability to connect directly with others can be a valuable tool in the helping professions. People who are empaths are often marvelous in dealing with others. They make excellent salespeople, ministers and therapists and function well in any role where their ability to feel what others feel would be of benefit.

Clairvoyance

Clairvoyance is the most commonly known psychic ability. It is the ability to foretell events that have not yet occurred or to see objects that are either far away or hidden to the normal perceptions. Clairvoyants often see spirits, guides or angels. Clairvoyance often gets confused with other psychic abilities and in my experience, is not as common as abilities that occur "in real time," such as most empathy and medical intuition. My own clairvoyance mostly comes in small ways: I'm given information not to take a certain road or certain path home and I always listen. I often find out after the fact that was an accident or a huge traffic delay on the route I intended to take.

Precognition, the ability to foresee events, may be considered a form of clairvoyance. I have talked about how strong negative energy transmits with greater distance and more force than positive energy and this is the case with the foreshadowing of events. As with my grandmother and the plane, I believe that precognition is available to many of us when someone who we love deeply is in danger, or we ourselves are in danger. It is not something that happens to me often, but there was one major instance I will never forget. Years before a horrible major urban disaster, I repeatedly "saw" the event, as if on a screen, but I had no idea about the causation or the timeframe. On the day the event occurred, I watched the news in shock with friends and relatives as my awful dream unfolded, with details exactly as they had appeared to me. Afterwards, I learned that many "light workers" saw the same visions. Since then, I work with other light workers following tragic events, natural or man-made, to help dispel the negative energy and help the healing process.

Retrocognition is the ability to see past lives. As karma affects us all, people often find it useful to do past life regression with someone who has the training to guide them along this path. Be sure you are working with someone who is knowledgeable and able to do this regression in a safe and skillful way.

Soul retrieval is a form of retrocognition through which one can reclaim a part of one's soul that has been lost in another lifetime with the aid of a skilled professional. It can be quite useful in healing difficult emotions that are not from this lifetime.

I think clairvoyance is the most desirable of the psychic abilities and certainly the one that's talked about the most. If you wish to develop your clairvoyance, active listening to the authentic voice is really the only way (we will discuss this topic in Chapter Eleven). It's quite difficult to create this ability, but you can exercise and develop it further. The most important thing is to realize that when it occurs, it's a true gift and needs to be treated with all the seriousness such a gift deserves.

Clairaudience

The type of clairvoyance related to hearing is called clairaudience. People with this ability can hear voices others cannot, either of their guides or other persons alive or passed. They may hear words or noises such as bells or even the channeling of guidance from other times or dimensions. The hearing of voices is not uncommon in religious experience. The question of whether someone is hearing his own voice or another voice (for instance, that of someone who has crossed over), will be also be discussed in Chapter Eleven.

Often people who have no other psychic experience have clairaudient ones. It occurs frequently after a loved one has died. They might hear their name being called or the name of their child, in the voice of the person who has passed. This common experience, in my opinion, is the departed person trying to communicate that they are okay now that they have crossed over to another world.

Clairalience

Clairalience is the ability to smell spiritual odors or aromas. Perhaps not quite as dramatic as hearing a voice, the ability to smell things is often quite helpful in spiritual work. When I am speaking to someone who has died, I often notice her perfume or his cologne first. It's like the experience of someone walking into a room. You recognize them by their scent. Every human being has a unique smell; it can be a key way to identify a spirit.

Some smells indicate danger. Clairalient people often smell smoke before a fire occurs or they sense a strong thunderstorm and smell the ozone before the lightning comes.

Clairkinesis

Clairkinesis is the ability to physically feel the presence of people or animals that have passed or of guides and angels. It can be perceived by both parties. Spirits may contact us by softly touching us on the shoulder or brushing their hand across our face. This occurrence is a common way for those who have crossed over to connect with us, and people who are sensitive and have this ability are quite blessed.

Clairsentience

Those with the gift of clairsentience are able to sense subtle feelings or energy or to know facts that are not easily known. This general term is used for seeing things like auras or chakras in people's bodies. Those with this ability often say that there are changes in the subtle energies with illness and health. For example, when I am looking at someone who has a heart problem, I often see discoloration of their heart chakra; it may look dark or brown or blackish, as opposed to a healthy green or rose.

General Intuition

General intuition refers to the psychic ability to know anything that cannot be known by our five senses, to just know things that you could not possibly know. General intuition covers anything that isn't described elsewhere. It can be independent of the other psychic abilities. A good example of this is the driving situation we mentioned earlier, of knowing someone's looking at you when you're on the road.

Channeling

One who is able to channel uses the above skills to allow an individual, spirit or person who has passed to use them as a conduit or as I like to say about myself, a "radio" that receives messages. Sometimes the message can be very esoteric, sometimes it is specific advice or guidance.

Many excellent channelers are out there. Many people are familiar with the "Abraham" messages; these spiritual teachings of love, joy and the law of attraction are from an entity on another plane.[2] An entity can choose a body that is on this plane as a channel through which to deliver messages. Channeling is very exciting and interesting. It requires the ability to turn off your own mind and allow another being's mind to take over yours, quite an extraordinary and interesting concept. Many times, people use substances to help them channel. Peyote has been used by native peoples, as have many other psychotropic drugs, but drugs are not necessary to channel. Some people will channel family members or others who have crossed over. Channelers are able to communicate with beings on the other side. These beings can provide specific information for people who request their guidance.

If channeling is an area where you have some ability or interest, it is important to work with a skilled practitioner to learn safe and effective methods.

Energy Healing

Energy healing is a broad term encompassing many forms of natural techniques whose purpose is to bring the body into a balanced state. Practitioners of the many forms of such healing are skilled in moving subtle energy and can, in fact, influence the organs and fluids of the body, releasing blocked energy. When stuck energy is shifted, the body naturally moves toward a state of balance and health. The question in regard to energy healing is whether the practitioner is moving something with his or her mind as in psychokinesis, or is channeling higher power through the crown chakra and hands, into the body that is being healed. Reiki practitioners, for example, acknowledge that they are not the healer, but have received attunements that allow healing energy to come through them.

---

[2] Abraham-Hicks Publications

Craniosacral work, homeopathy, polarity and many other forms of energy healing require varying degrees of training and knowledge about the physical body, as well as an ability to still the mind and focus. It may even be said that many practitioners of the healing arts, including mainstream doctors and surgeons, might be channeling at times, receiving guidance as to the best techniques and methods to use with a particular person. You probably know the feeling of an exceptionally good massage. The therapist seems to be "listening" to your body, coaxing and working your muscles and joints in exactly the manner and the location they need in order to release tension. The most effective practitioners are often those who use their intuitive sense (whether they acknowledge it or not) in addition to technique.

Our strong desire to heal and be healed is a powerful force and can evoke aid from sources beyond our knowing.

I have a deep respect for energy healing. I have seen it work both when I use it and when I receive it. Our strong desire to heal and be healed is a powerful force in itself and can evoke aid from sources beyond our knowing.

Whether you consider it a form of psychokinesis or a form of channeling energies from another force, a higher power—energy healing is a vital field of exploration and enormous benefit.

Telepathy

Telepathy is the ability to read minds. It is quite rare. Because I can feel people's feelings, they often mistake my ability as telepathy. I cannot hear someone's thoughts, but can interpret the feelings. Telepathy is a gift I am glad not to have. I think it would make life very troubling to hear the random musings going on in people's minds and those with this gift are often troubled greatly by it.

Telekinesis/Psychokinesis

Telekinesis is the ability to move or alter physical objects using your mind. I personally have never been able to move anything very heavy, but you may remember my practice as a youngster of moving the suspended rubber ball. It is interesting because it's the physical manifestation of using psychic and energetic power to do physical activities.

Psychometry

Psychometry allows us to understand a person through the objects they have touched or through photographs. Objects retain the vibration of the owner, especially well-worn things like wedding rings, etc.

An interesting and well-known example of psychometry is the method by which the Dalai Lama is chosen, or more aptly, found. The Fourteenth Dalai Lama, considered to be a reincarnation of his predecessor, was discovered by a centuries-old tradition that includes psychometry. The High Lamas followed visions and signs to find the child who they felt was the new Dalai Lama. The two-year-old underwent several tests and assessments, the main one involving the identification of objects belonging to his predecessor. When presented with a number of objects such as prayer beads and a bell that were possessions of the previous Dalai Lama, along with similar items that were not, the boy instantly identified the correct ones, saying, "It's mine. It's mine."

Aura Reading

Those who can read auras have the ability to see the energy field around a person. Much can be known about a person's health and well-being from this technique. When I teach a class in expanding psychic ability, I often pair people up and ask them to draw their partner's aura and chakras. Crayons or colored pencils are a big help. The color and where they reside in the body are very useful. We will have the opportunity to practice this ability in a later chapter.

Medical Intuition

Medical intuition is a type of psychic ability that allows someone to see, albeit to different degrees, illness and wellness within the body of a person or an animal. In my case, I see the organs, blood, connective tissue and bone as if I am looking at actual living bodies. To me, it appears as if I can actually see inside the skin. Once, a cute little sixteen-year-old girl asked if I could see her underwear. No one had ever asked me that before, and I found it very amusing. She was quite upset at the thought so I said to her, "Honestly, I find what's inside you much more interesting than your underwear."

Medical intuitives vary greatly in what they are able to see. Some see blockages of energies around chakras and don't see specific organs at all. Others may see dark clouds or shadows over areas that are affected in the body. One of my pet peeves is that not all medical intuitives study anatomy and physiology. They may feel that they do not need to. I have been trying to address this lack of medical expertise for a very long time and will continue to do so. If you don't know anatomy and physiology, then looking at a body and seeing that something is wrong is less useful.

The Undetected Problem: A Tall Tale

When I started out and hung my shingle as a medical intuitive, a woman came to see me because she could not recover from a debilitating injury. She was a private detective, about six feet tall and told me she did not believe in me and didn't think that anything I would say could be true. She was required to see me because she was disabled and her company couldn't believe that she was still in pain. Somehow she was referred to me; I was her last chance to find out what was wrong before she was unemployed and living on disability.

She had been on a stakeout sitting in her car in the dark with the lights off near a tollbooth. Another car pulled off the road and as it was the middle of the night, the driver didn't see her and crashed into her car at a high speed. She was taken to the hospital where an MRI was performed, showing only minor problems. Yet she was in terrible pain.

This was a really easy one for me. The minute she walked in I had noticed that her back was terribly injured. I couldn't understand why the MRI had not picked up this injury, so I asked her, "What sections of your body did they do an MRI on?" She informed me that they did a head and neck MRI. The injuries that I saw were much lower down in the thoracic spine. I said, "Well, you're a very tall person. Injuries that you might receive from hitting the steering wheel would affect your midsection. Go back and tell them to MRI your thoracic area, because you have some cracked vertebrae which are probably pinching nerves and causing you pain."

She went away and never let me know what happened. (That's another one of my pet peeves by the way—people not letting me know what happens after I see them.) One day, I happened to see her on the street. She told me that I had been correct. The doctors found the cracks in her vertebrae where I had indicated and she was given the appropriate treatment and physical therapy. She went back to work. She also informed me that she still didn't believe in me and thought I made a lucky guess. I can live with that. After all, detectives live according to logic and she couldn't explain what happened!

The fun part of the story is that she told me that the gentleman who came over to help her after the crash was one of the tollbooth operators and they were planning to marry in the next several weeks. I was waiting for an invitation to the wedding but it never came.

Mediumship

The ability to speak to people who have crossed over is actually a psychic ability we all have. It's not really a paranormal ability. It's just that some people have it to a greater degree than others and they exercise it. It takes real stillness of mind to connect with people who have passed. And it takes a lot of trust to believe that they are actually communicating with you, but they can and do. I would encourage you to try to communicate with people who you have lost and with whom you wish to maintain a relationship.

I wish I could give you logical, factual information about what's "out there," but all I can really do is share my construct. My belief is that a part of us, some call it our soul, continues throughout our lifetime and transfers after we die to incarnate in another being. I believe that we are on a path with goals to achieve and lessons to learn from each of these lifetimes. I also believe that ultimately we reach a point where we no longer have to continue to live these lifetimes in order to learn our lessons and at that point, we reach a place that some might call heaven, others might call Nirvana.

The ability to speak to people who have crossed over is actually a psychic ability we all have.

Many cultures revere and connect with ancestors as guides and helpers. You may wonder why we can still contact someone if they have indeed reincarnated. The reason is because we exist in several dimensions simultaneously and we may leave part of ourselves in a certain dimension in order to help those still in physical form.

I'm not asking you to believe what I believe or to have the same constructs. I didn't really want to believe that I could talk to dead people for a very long time. But I find that I know things that it would be impossible for me to know unless I was communicating with a person on the other side. So it's clear to me that such communication is real. We have all seen those movies with the séance and the fainting lady. I don't think that either the séance or the fainting is required.

Sounds like a good time for a ghost story.

The Strange Bedfellow

My favorite story regarding this subject is of a young woman who came to me seeking to be rid of her "ghost." Her priest sent her to me because she was being haunted, something the Catholic Church has more skill and experience in dealing with than I do, but no longer deals with very often. So this Boston priest sends his people in need of exorcism to a nice Jewish girl in the suburbs.

This woman's ghost, as she explained, was a man who was with her all of the time. He even got into bed with her. She would feel a rush of air on her face, and then actually feel the bed sink down next to her when she was going to sleep. The ghost had recently started to turn lights on and off in her house, and actually knocked over a lamp, greatly disturbing her young child. After three years, during which time he even traveled with her, she wanted him gone. Her boyfriend felt that there was a third party in the relationship!

I asked her to do a little prayer with me and we invited the spirit in. I could see him rather clearly and was able to get his first and last names, unusual for me, and then sent my client home with the assignment of finding out who he was and if he had lived at her address.

She returned a few weeks later. It turned out that the ghost was indeed a man who had lived in her apartment. His wife had died there, and he had subsequently committed suicide in the bedroom. Often a "ghost" becomes "stuck"

if he dies suddenly or by suicide. A part of this person gets stuck in this dimension and he is confused and disoriented, in a state of suspension.[3]
(The term "spirit" is a more general term for people who have crossed over.)

We invited the ghost back and explained that my client was not his wife and that he needed to move on so that he could be with his wife. We did a crossing-over ceremony for him which went very well. *Job done, I thought,* although my client seemed a bit upset. I received a check from her the following week, but to my surprise, it bounced. When I called her she said, "I want him back, I miss him." I told her that she could communicate with "her ghost" through her prayers, and to please send another check. But I never heard from her again.

Mediumship gets a lot of bad press, but it has always provided a very important service. It allows us to communicate and gain wisdom from those who have passed and maintains the continuity of generations.

Business Intuition

Called "trusting your gut" as my colleague Lynn Robinson teaches in her terrific books and lectures[4], business intuition is a whole field of teaching forward-looking enterprises how to harness the psychic and intuitive abilities of the staff for the good of the company and its employees. It is no surprise that the Japanese are way ahead of us in this regard and that Lynn often speaks to them about harnessing this wonderful energy.

Animal Communication

Despite my cat experience, I am not an animal communicator, although I think it is a noble task. From "horse whispering" to getting Fido to stop peeing in the corner, talking to our four-legged friends is a wonderful thing. Amazing behavioral and spiritual results are possible from the work of those with this ability. Many veterinarians are clandestine animal communicators.

Lucid and Other Dreaming

People have been interpreting dreams as long as there have been people to dream them. Strictly from a psychological point of view, sleep is the place where we process the things that we aren't able to process during the course of our day.

---

[3] Most of the time ghosts can't hurt you. Hollywood movies notwithstanding, usually all ghosts can do is create a little breeze, open doors or do small actions that don't require a lot of energetic force. I have never seen a ghost pick up a knife, or anything of that nature.

[4] Robinson, Lynn. Trust Your Gut: How the Power of Intuition Can Grow Your Business. Kaplan Publishing.

These dreams can have a deeper meaning and can often be psychic in nature, even prophetic.

Many people experience their psychic abilities in their dreams. If you believe that you are a person with this ability, it's a good idea to keep a dream journal. Because dreams are so fleeting, it's important to keep this journal (or other recording method) right by your bed. Record your dreams for a month if you can, as accurately as you remember them. Do this recording without interpreting them. Then go back at the end of a month and see if there is more meaning than you realized at the time, whether events were predicted or people acted in ways foreshadowed by your dreams.

Lucid dreaming is an interesting concept. It is similar to the ability to leave your body and do astral travel; only this travel is done in your sleep. When you are having a lucid dream, you might think you are awake, get up and walk to the refrigerator or walk out a window into the sky and see your neighbors, etc. People who are into lucid dreaming make a consistent effort to cultivate this ability.

If you feel you might want to explore this area, start your dream journal. There are even programs you can get for your smart phone that will give you wave signals to stimulate lucid dreaming.

All of these abilities are a part of our lives to a greater or lesser extent. Remember that training with a skilled spiritual teacher is the safest, surest way to progress on your path. They will guide you toward your areas of strength and help you decide how best to use them to benefit yourself and others.

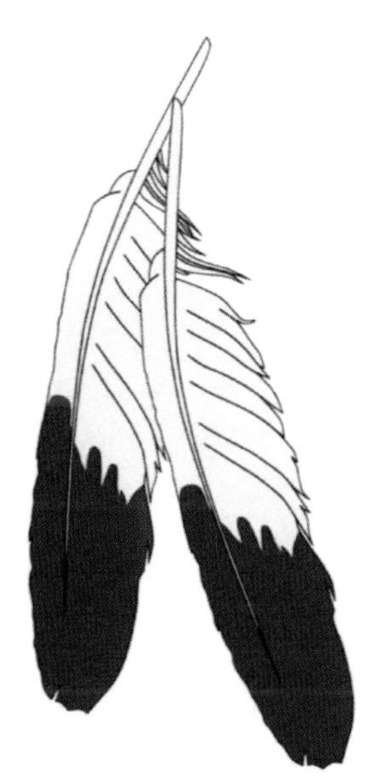

PART TWO

Cornerstones of a Spiritual Practice

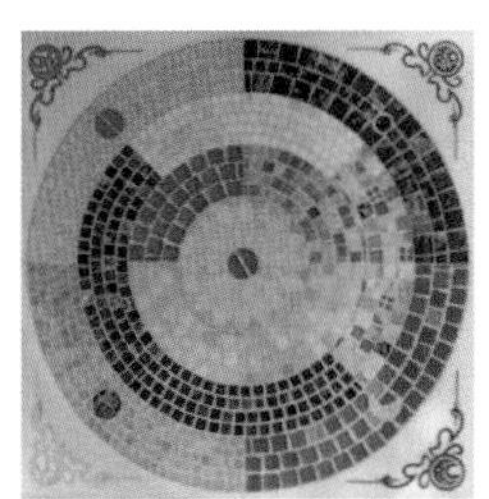

Cornerstones of a Spiritual Practice

Cornerstones of a spiritual practice are essential to beginning your journey toward a freer and more vibrant spiritual life. They are: intention, creating a sacred space, shielding, de-cording, meditation and listening for the authentic voice. All are important aspects of moving forward and regardless of how you wish to practice your spirituality; if you do not learn these essential first steps everything else will be more difficult. They go by many names, but I chose these simple terms to help free us of the jargon or specifics of any particular religious practice. Often people go to retreats to learn these skills, but I offer these simple beginning steps to allow the openness required for any and all paths. It does not matter very much which religious group you choose to follow; these elements are present in all.

For example, it is typical to do a Vision Quest in many Native American cultures. A rite of passage that takes place alone in the wilderness, the Vision Quest shows a person that they can become strong and quiet in nature and can begin to learn to listen to inner and outer guidance. It's the process of creating openness and staying within your own thoughts, fears and hopes.

Other traditions use repeated prayers or mantras to provide a meditative state, either alone or in groups allowing Spirit to become an integral part of a person's makeup. Nuns and priests choose a cloistered order to create the space within themselves for God and the Light. Jews take many fast days to quiet the mind from everyday thoughts of food and socializing to allow time with God. Many forms of yoga are used in a similar manner. All of these practices are good and useful means to the ends we are seeking. I'm sure you can think of many examples of such contemplative practices. You can do the same thing by creating the space within yourself without leaving your warm and cozy home.

We will cover each of the cornerstones in more depth, but I would like to quickly introduce each of them here:

Intention is the spiritual "glue" that connects your thoughts and actions and underlies your practice and your commitment to make conscious choices for the highest good of all.

A *sacred space* allows you to create a place to become your spiritual self instantly and without interruption.

Shielding protects us from the negative thoughts and energies of others, intended or not.

De-cording is the process of removing old, no longer useful connections that may harm us if left unpruned.

Meditation quiets the mind and body and allows time for openness to information and peace.

Learning to hear your authentic voice teaches how to know the difference between your own agenda and what is being taught to you by your guides and the spirit world.

CHAPTER SIX

Intention

We are buffeted by fate, burdened by responsibility, moved by love, and blessed with joy. We do things incorrectly, our comments are misconstrued, our actions questioned—these things we cannot control. What we can control, perhaps the *only* thing we can control, is our intention. We do have total control of what we are trying to do, to create or to be. Not setting intentions is not living a conscious life; it is just reacting to circumstances, never making choices. Having intention is being proactive, not reactive.

Making a Conscious Choice

Who you are and where you have been in life are not important in the concept of intention. We all have done noble things and we have all made terrible mistakes; that is being human. What I am hoping you take from this book is that no matter what your circumstances, you have choices. One of the most important is defining who you want to be going forward. It doesn't matter whether you are 12 or 120; you still have control of your intention and what you put out to the Universe. All spirituality is about intention and how we act upon it with our behavior.

All spirituality is about intention and how we act upon it with our behavior.

Most people live reacting from event to event. Something happens: you lose a job, injure your body, or receive a promotion. In response, you decide how to look for a new job, how to heal your body or how to celebrate your promotion. We can control some variables in our life—working hard, being careful about our bodies, eating well and exercising will go a long way toward getting us a better life. But unless you clearly set your intentions, you're blowing in the wind. You are taking no control and being reactive to events. Sometimes events are unavoidable: you are involved in a car crash, you experience healing or someone harms you from out of the blue. But the rest is up to you. How you conduct yourself and whether it is with intention and grace is your responsibility.

Hopefully, in the course of creating your spiritual practice, you will set the intention of becoming a more spiritual person, being conscious of your actions and how they ripple out and flow to others, both human and otherwise. Additionally, you will chart a course of becoming a person working for the Light. Let your intention remain your internal compass. It doesn't matter what your beliefs, politics or personal history are, or whether you are reading this book from a jail cell or a monastery. What I hope is that going forward you will choose to do good in all of your actions, and you will move with the intention of benefitting the planet and the living beings upon it.

What does it mean to be a person working for the Light? "Light worker" is a phrase commonly used to describe someone who sets a conscious intention to change the world for the better. You might teach children, initiate recycling in your community or simply conduct your life in a way that benefits all beings. Light workers are all over the world, and perhaps all over the universe. You become one by remaining aware and awake to all the ways you can illuminate the world around you. In any job and any environment, you can create Light by putting your intention into action. I hope that by the end of this book, you will have made the commitment to work in the Light by sending positive energy wherever healing is needed, whether at home or in the world.

Let your intention remain your internal compass.

Sometimes it is very hard to let go of the ego or self and allow the greater good to surface. Your spiritual exercises will help you to slow down and take the time to set intention. Meditation, prayers and all of the cornerstones of your practice will allow space for setting intentions. Do you want to be an observer of your life or do you want to take control? Intention is about taking control.

Intention should never be used to harm another. If someone is doing harmful things, then of course you want to be responsible and step in or call the authorities if necessary. But you should never set intention of revenge or to cause pain. That is not to say we live without anger. As much as I would like to believe I can do so, I have certainly become angry. But it is what you do with that anger that matters. Anger can be an important signal, as I will discuss in the chapter about negative emotions. But taking that anger and making it a blessing... that is good. The Dalai Lama says "everyone is our mother."[5] Try to remember that bad behavior often comes from pain or evil, and the counter to both is to shed your Light upon it.

You are probably reading this book as someone who has a gift; we all do. Without positive intentions, however, the gift will remain fallow and may even cause symptoms or dark thoughts. Using your abilities properly can be quite healing, so I encourage you to embrace them and use them for the greater good.

---

[5] His Holiness the Dalai Lama, The Art of Happiness, Riverhead.

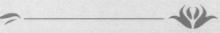

INTENTION

Imagine that someone has done you wrong. They took credit for your work at the office. You are furious. What do you do?

Close your eyes. Take several calming breaths.

Go into your feelings. Acknowledge them but do not engage. Setting your intention for the highest good of all, allow all the negatives to release.

Think: what is the best outcome here?

List your options. Often the answer is to conduct yourself in a loving way to the person who wronged you.

Think about how you appear to others coming from a place of calm versus spluttering and spitting. Think about intention and how it informs this decision.

CHAPTER SEVEN

Creating a Sacred Space

Another cornerstone of your spiritual journey is making a sacred space for yourself. This might not sound like one of the most important things that you are going to do on your journey, but believe me it is essential. You must have a safe, private space where you can meditate or just calm and restore yourself. The creation of this space is the setting of an intention that you will dedicate a part of your life and a significant amount of your time to your spiritual development. It is the physical manifestation of that dedication so it is quite important.

Your Inner Environment

In order to create a sacred space you must choose an environment. Often that environment will be a place in your home and we will talk about how to create that place. But you must also create a sacred space in your mind—a destination to travel from for your journey. It will be the beginning point, your home base, as it were. Think about places that have significance to you, perhaps a place you went on vacation or even a tree that you liked to sit under when you were a child. This will always be a safe space that you can return to from your journeys, a place that allows you to come back safely into the world. It will become a portal.

I have several inner sacred spaces. I find that for different kinds of journeying I choose to go from different starting points. One of my favorite spaces is at the junction of two rivers in Vermont, in the middle of the woods. It's very quiet. This place is where I went for my vision quest. I often use this starting point when I am looking to expand my view of something. I have another safe space for working on issues that are personal, a place that is warm and cuddly and has lots of soft pillows and cushions, a place where I can feel absolutely safe and at home.

When I return to it, I feel nurtured and warm. I often use the Wolf as my guide, and for journeys where I want to walk with the wolf, I will start in the wolf den surrounded by my litter mates, warm and cozy. From that place I can walk to many worlds.

Your sacred space can be any place that you choose in your mind. It can either be an actual place, or one that you create and visualize. Some people like to create a sacred space sitting beside one of their guides. This space will become very important for you as you journey. This is your interior sacred space, as opposed to your exterior sacred space which we will talk about next.

So let's move on to your home.

Creating an Altar

To create your physical sacred space, you will need to create an altar. The actual altar need not be one that is like the altar in your church or place of worship. It can be a bookshelf, a dresser top or any place that will not be touched by other people. It can even be a window sill.

On this altar, you will place a collection of objects that have strong meaning for you. They can be anything that evokes feelings of peace or spirituality. For example, if you had a wonderful trip where you sat on the beach and contemplated your place in the world, you might have collected some shells. Every time you looked at those shells, your mind would be brought back to that time, the pleasant feeling and the gentle waves. This memory creates a meditative moment. Your altar should have objects on it that evoke these kinds of moments.

An altar is not a stagnant thing. It is a living representation of where your spirituality resides at any given time.

Your altar is also a good place for pictures or statues of significant deities or spiritual people. You might find that Jesus and Buddha are quite happy to be seated side by side. It is also nice to place some photos of ancestors, children and grandchildren there; these images help to remind you of the continuity of life. Anything that works for you is good.

People also change their altars depending on where they are in their lives. An altar is not a stagnant thing. It is a living representation of where your spirituality resides at any given time.

Your altar should be in a place that no one else touches. One woman I know shares a small apartment with several people. She purchased a shoji screen and blocked off a corner just large enough for a comfortable chair, a sitting cushion and her altar. That is sufficient, as long as it feels like your personal and sacred space.

Your sacred space should be quiet in order to meditate. I've even seen some people remodel broom closets. It needs to be a refuge, a home for your soul.

Sacred Objects

As your altar becomes a focal point for your spiritual growth, the objects placed here become sacred objects because you make them so by your intention. You are dedicating them to this time and space for your spiritual work.

Let's look at some of the helpful items and tools you might use on your altar.

Smudge

A regular part of your sacred space is smudging, which is the use of certain plants or their essences to cleanse and purify a place or a person. The ritual of smudging is both symbolic and physical; certain herbs can purify the air both literally and energetically with their scent or their smoke. We need to cleanse and refresh our space, because we all leave "energy signatures" behind us whether we want to or not (that is where ghosts come from). These energy signatures are emotions that can affect others and sometimes can be very strong, so it is a good idea to smudge. If, for instance, someone comes to your home and you feel a dark energy or have a negative interaction, you can cleanse the space this way. In fact, you might consider smudging on a regular basis as part of your housecleaning routine.

Traditionally, what people used for smudge depended on the herbs that were available in that part of the world. Most smudges in the western world tend to have sage in them. The frankincense in my smudge is a very rare tree resin that was said to be one of the gifts that the three wise men gave to the baby Jesus. I have been told that some native cultures in the Arctic use smudge that contains the blubber of whales. I have a friend who uses witch hazel as a smudge. I think she is probably the most pragmatic, as that is the most inexpensive way to smudge I've ever heard of.

Just as I smudge my office between each person's visit to clear the air for the next person, you can clear the air for yourself. You will need a feather to "brush" the air and distribute the scent. I happen to have a lovely handmade smudging feather that was given to me as a gift, but you can pick up a feather from the ground that a bird has gifted you and it will be just as effective. Smudge is traditionally burned, but as I work with a lot of people with allergies and breathing problems, it's not practical for me to use a smudge that requires burning, so I use a liquid spray smudge. Also, I am afraid of setting a fire by leaving something that might still be smoldering. I take my feather, spray the smudge on it and "brush" the air with it. At the end of a client session, I usually smudge them as well. I circle the air around the top of their energy body and smudge around their physical body (the "yolk" inside the "egg"), and I smudge around where the "shell" or aura would be.

Just a little safety note: if you are burning an herb such as sage, you may light it in a fireproof dish, or use the more traditional clamshell (or purchase a bundle and light the tip). Proceed to waft the smoke. Just be certain that herbs are completely extinguished when you are done.

You might consider smudging on a regular basis as part of your housecleaning routine.

If you use different kinds of smudge you will get different experiences, so it's important to try different things and see what resonates for you. You might find that you like a particular scent, or that a certain scent upsets you. Clearly, it must make you feel good in order to clear the energy in your world. You can even create your own blend. No particular formula is going to work better than another. I assume that if you really want to, you could probably smudge with commercial spray air freshener, which would not be my choice, but I think it could be as valid as any other smudge, as it is all about the intention of clearing.

I mentioned that I smudge after every person who visits my office. I do that so that each new person has her own unique experience without having to deal with the residual energy left by another. My clients often say that the environment is very calming and peaceful. I have worked to make it so, and a large part of that is due to the fact that I smudge so consistently.

Stones and Crystals

You may choose stones for your sacred space, stones that you pick up in your travels or perhaps stones or crystals that are used to support the different chakras. Crystals have been used ever since people started digging them out of the earth. They are valued as sale and trade objects and, of course, as ornamentation. Because certain colors are associated with each of the chakras, it is believed that crystals of these colors can aid in healing of the spirit, mind and body. For example, green colored stones are often associated with the heart and are believed to have a calming effect when worn. Blue stones are associated with the throat and are said to assist in

healing that area by supporting speech. Often when I'm going to speak in public, I will wear turquoise. Turquoise is believed to affect both the heart chakra and throat chakra, so it strengthens my heart and the ability to speak effectively from my heart. Rose quartz is another common choice as an altar object or as jewelry because it, too, supports heart energy and is considered a love-generating crystal.

Often people carry a little pouch containing the crystals that they feel they need. You might carry a stone representing the chakra(s) that you feel needs strengthening. See the reading list at the end of this book for reference to an excellent work on crystals, the many different types and how they affect both humans and animals.

Sacred Sound and Light

Drum. Many people like to use drumming in their sacred space. Drums can create the feeling of a heartbeat, which is very calming. If you are the kind of person that likes to drum, I would encourage you to buy a natural skin or similar organic material drum. If you are vegan, there are certain kinds of paper drums that work just as well and sound quite wonderful; they are also significantly less expensive. A drum does not have to be fancy to provide what you need.

Singing bowl. You can get these at Tibetan stores or online. They are often made of brass or crystal and create a beautiful ringing tone that is said to imitate the "ohm" sound, the universal sacred sound. These bowls come in various sizes and notes of the scale.

Audio recordings, music or nature sounds. If you are not inclined to beat a drum or play a bell yourself, it's perfectly fine to use a soundtrack of drumming, bells, or chanting. I am particularly fond of Gregorian chant, and find it a wonderful background to my meditation practice. Use your imagination; music has been used in many ways to create sacred space. I suppose it is possible to use loud rock music but that's not something that I would encourage, as it is distracting. The music should be of a background nature, not in the foreground.

Some people like the sound of waves crashing on the beach, or running water. You can also purchase a small fountain if you like that sound and use it in your sacred space.

Light. Light is just as important as sound in your sacred space. If you like candles, use the candlelight to bring its own element of fire into the space. Soft lighting of any kind can be effective or you may like to imitate bright daylight. Some people choose different color lights to create different kinds of environments. Colored bulbs can help you make a sacred space in any environment. Choose a color that resonates with your feelings.

The most important factor in the creation of your sacred space is that you have an environment that has sound, light and feelings around you that are safe, secure and private.

CHAPTER EIGHT

Shielding

Now that you are creating a safe place for meditation and journeying, you should also learn to protect yourself energetically in the world. Shielding is a way of protecting ourselves from the assaults of emotion, tension and negative energy we may encounter. It is essential that we develop the ability to shield effectively, so I teach it to all of my students. We must be protected in order to continue a spiritual practice. If you do so without protection, you take the risk of random negative emotions entering your field and negative energies affecting your energetic balance.

Group Practice

The following story will give you a sense of how shielding can make a difference in your life and your work. A lovely woman, a psychologist who was working with end-stage cancer patients, came to me for an intuitive body scan because she was concerned that she might have cancer. She worked every day with people who were very close to death and the energy around her was affecting her feelings about her health and her own well-being. I duly scanned her body, and told her that no, she did not have cancer, but she was holding a lot of stress in her body and was receiving the energy of people around her who had very negative feelings and thoughts. Many of those thoughts were fear and anger, which are very easily transmitted and can harm others, especially those who are working closely with these emotions and the people having them.

I asked her if she understood the concept of shielding. She had never heard of it, so I taught her the method that I will be teaching you. She implemented it and for the most part, had no problem continuing to work with the challenging population she had chosen to serve. She was able to feel healthy and strong where those around her were not. She could do her job effectively, remain open and helpful to those who needed her and also remain strong in her own body and energy field.

Shortly after our meeting, a co-worker of hers came to me with the same problem. She was distraught and concerned for her health and felt stressed all the time. She, too, was concerned that her health was deteriorating and perhaps she might have cancer, although that was not the case either. I also taught her the technique of shielding. When a third person from the clinic called, I asked her how many people worked at the clinic and she told me there were nine. I said, "Well, we might as well get together, do a shielding workshop and save everyone some time and money." We did and had a lovely evening. As far as I know, the problem was resolved and they were all able to do their jobs effectively and with protection.

A person doesn't have to intend you harm in order for you to require shielding from their negative thoughts and energies.

This situation is a classic example of people who were affected by their work environment, but were not aware of it. It happens all of the time, and can occur in your work environment or your home. A person doesn't have to intend you harm in order for you to require shielding from their negative thoughts and energies. Our best resource to thrive is by providing ourselves with effective shielding.

Creating Your Energy Shield

How do we create a shield? We do it by making a protective energy field around ourselves. Practically speaking, a shield is a way to bring protective energy into and around your energy body. It covers you from above your head to under your feet, front and back. It encompasses you without blocking movement. A shield does not allow in negative energy, but does allow in positive energy. We create our shield the same way we approach all of our spiritual work: using our intention and focusing on a result that is for the highest good.

What does an energy shield look like? We each get to create our own. To give you an idea of what an energy shield is, let me tell you what mine looks like. Do you remember Maxwell Smart's "cone of silence?" There was a silly TV series called "Get Smart" when I was young. Whenever Max needed to speak privately, he would call down his cone of silence. It looked like a large, clear bell jar that surrounded his body. I adapted my conceptual shield to look this way. I use this shield every day in my work. It helps me to deal with the energy that people bring into my space and keeps me from absorbing their physical or emotional negativity.

You can create a simple shield by just surrounding yourself with white light—a basic shield. I find that a more personalized protective shield is even better. I love to hear the ideas people come up with for their shields. They express someone's unique view of the world and their quirky personality characteristics. They can be very specific. My clients and students have been imaginative in making their shields out of many different materials: fabric, woven leather, steel, plexiglas and glass. It is important that you create a shield that feels personally comfortable. One woman created a beautiful feather cape, another used a trench coat and one gentleman I worked with used a tent. Anything that makes you feel protected will work. It must be an image that feels good to you and makes you feel safe.

It may sound like some imaginary game, but you are actually creating a field around your body. This field is as real as anything that can be seen or touched and it can indeed protect you. It can't protect you against bullets or knives, but it can protect you against attacks from others that are emotional or energetic in nature. Whether in your work environment, your home or anywhere else, remember that a person does not have to intend you harm in order for you to require shielding from their negative thoughts and emotions.

Let your imagination go and create your own personal shield. You might like to try the exercises at the end of this chapter.

Mauled at the Mall

Have you ever had the experience of being in a crowded area such as a subway station or a shopping mall and felt a wave of exhaustion or maybe even stress in the presence of a group of people? In a place like a mall or any enclosed place, we are often subject to the energy that is sent from individuals and is bouncing around because it has no way to escape.

It used to be that whenever I went into a large space like a mall, I would feel exhausted after just a few minutes. A typical mall is an enclosed space with no windows, very little natural light and recirculated air. For someone who is sensitive to energy, it can be a very dangerous place. Until I realized what was happening to me in malls, I would feel drained and somehow a bit "bruised" after about half an hour of walking around. Think about it: in a mall there are lots of people who are feeling all kinds of strong emotions. There are people who are angry, excited, confused or behaving unpredictably. This energy has nowhere to go; the negative feelings just ricochet around. Outdoor environments are less problematic because there is a lot of space for energy to dissipate; a mall enclosure is the exact opposite.

If you've felt uneasy, drained or distressed being in a mall or similar environment, you are probably a person who is sensitive to this type of energy, and should only go into to such places shielded. Not shielding in such an environment can not only tire you and weaken your body, it can actually affect your immune system. Just think about how many adolescents walk around the mall with storm clouds of emotions around them. Multiply those feelings by hundreds of people and that should convince you that it's probably a good idea to be shielded in a mall.

Surprisingly, I am not bothered by a movie theater (although I know it affects some people). One reason may be that everyone's energy is facing in the same direction, so I try to sit at the back of the theater where the energy is not directed toward me. It may also be that the audience is distracted by the movie and their energy is focused and drawn to the screen, not toward others around them.

Your Environments Affect You

Become conscious of your environments and how you feel. You will become aware that certain environments are safer than others. We talked about creating a safe space in your home, but it is equally important to create a safe space at your workplace and other places that you frequent regularly. Did you ever notice that people are often very attached to their car environments? They establish a little world within their cars with their bottles of water, cups of coffee, accessories, personal electronic devices, even videos. Our car is a small environment that we get to control very effectively. We have a little space where we have a great degree of say about what goes into it, and the energy is usually ours or that of people with whom we are close.

Think about this concept of personal space in the other areas of your life. For instance, we don't often have a lot of choice in the place where we work. Folks who work in cubicles often have a problem controlling the energy around them. If you think about it, this kind of office environment is like a mall with little boxed off spaces in it. All the problems of a large mall area exist, but with the false appearance of privacy.

Just because an area is familiar does not mean you don't have to be shielded in it. Sometimes the most familiar environments can be the places that drain our energy the most, so it's a good idea to take a serious look at your environment, both at work and at home. I know that you are accustomed to the energy of these places, but if you look with a critical eye, you will realize that certain places feel less comfortable than others. They may make you tired or stressed or you may find that a specific part of your body reacts to these spaces. If a specific part of your body feels stressed, you should consider double shielding or extra shielding that area. If you have a difficult boss or difficult coworkers, you need to be shielded at work. If you have no choice but to be in certain places and cannot change the environment itself, the shield is an effective tool.

If you have no choice but to be in certain places and cannot change the environment itself, the shield is an effective tool.

Keep an eye out when you are in new environments and notice the way that your body and mind react. For example, I used to have to go into City Hall for my work, where there was enormous frustration and much locked-in energy. I would never have thought before I studied energy work that this environment, where I was a stranger and nobody knew me, could be so damaging. Yet each time I went there, I felt physically ill when I left. Your vigilance in this matter is very important. You must be protected in order to function effectively.

CREATING YOUR ENERGY SHIELD

Think about what you want your shield to look like. Imagine what you would put around you that would make you feel protected and safe and would also let you move freely and go about your business.

Take some time to think about what might work for you. (Remember that your shield must cover your entire auric body, so it must go above your head and below your feet, back and front.)

Once you come up with the image of your shield, try it on. See how it feels around your body and make adjustments where necessary.

TESTING YOUR SHIELD

When you have designed your shield, tried it on and have become comfortable with it, it's time to try it out. For this exercise you will need to enlist a friend who is interested in creating his own shield.

Once you have both created your shields, gently create an "energy" foam ball in your mind and, using your mind, throw it at your friend's shield.

Picture very carefully what part of the body you are throwing into. Don't throw it at the eyes or places that might do damage; throw it at the arms or legs. If the shield is working, they will probably feel where the energy hits but it will not feel harmful.

Change roles and have them do the same with you.

When I am training students I gradually work with heavier and larger objects but for our purposes here, I think that it's probably better to stick with the foam ball.

I use my shield every day. I put it on as I would clothing when I begin my work. I have to take it off at times in order to be open enough to do some of my work but I can open and close it very quickly as needed. I may do this many times during the course of a day. Once I have worked with someone and I know that her energy is safe for me, I can take my shield off. But until I am quite sure that I am no longer vulnerable, I leave it on. All this may sound quite strange to you, but as you become more aware of your energy body and continue to practice shielding, you will find it an indispensable tool.

In the next chapter, we will talk about another cornerstone of your spiritual practice. After you have created the shield and worked with it, you need to learn how to remove the harmful cords that connect you to others. This practice is called de-cording.

CHAPTER NINE

De-cording

Another fundamental practice I teach to students beginning a spiritual path is the housecleaning of old emotional issues. One of the most important ways to do this is to clear our energy body by a process called "de-cording." De-cording eliminates the emotional cords or connections to others that are unhealthy and that often slow down the progress of emptying ourselves of old, no longer useful energetic bonds. These bonds build up over the course of our lifetime and sap emotional energy needed for growth and strength.

We create a cord simply by having deep emotions and experiences with someone. We are corded to our bosses, partners, friends, enemies, siblings and perhaps even the tradespeople that we deal with on a regular basis. It would all be fine if everyone were emotionally healthy and there were no miscommunications, anger, fear or frustration. But because we don't live in a perfect world, we can cord in an unhealthy way.

I invite you to eliminate the cords that are not necessary to your existence. Why would you want to? Because we have only a certain amount of energy, psychic and otherwise, and we want to use that energy efficiently. If you were a computer and you were running really slowly, you might decide to remove the "cookies" that you weren't using to improve operating efficiency. De-cording is a way to improve your energy efficiency. Having too many cookies on your computer may not be dangerous, but having cords to people who can harm us may be dangerous indeed. All the energy we use thinking about old injustices or emotional damage blocks us from becoming the truly free and spiritually-directed people we would like to be.

There was an artist who died about ten years ago who made the most amazing pictures. His drawings and paintings showed people with lines connecting them from different parts of their bodies or their chakras. Some connections appeared healthy and mutually beneficial; others appeared to be strangling or tangled. We create a cord to anyone with whom we interact on an ongoing basis.

Cords may look like healthy red arteries or like an umbilical cord, a positive thing. (Our original cord, of course, is the umbilical cord; it attaches us to our mother and is the seat of the second chakra, our life force.) Or they may look like twisted wire or vines, rotted trees, and so on. I've heard a lot of different descriptions. Basically, anything that looks like it's not healthy probably isn't. A harmful cord isn't necessarily about an event, but it is usually a very strong feeling such as anger, embarrassment or frustration.

The "surgery" of cord-cutting is where the fun part comes in, as you get to choose an imaginary tool to cut the cord. (Being of a practical nature, I tend to use scissors but you can imagine whatever you like.) Then we may ask guides for help in removing unhealthy cords. Some people ask angels for help. One woman I know has the Acme Angel Service come in whenever she needs them.

The Ties That Bind

Let me give you an example of how cutting harmful cords can bring about healing. Liz is a woman in her early forties with a successful career who had returned to her mother's home to take care of her mother in the last stages of her life. This arrangement seems noble, and in most cases it is. But in this case it was not healthy for either Liz or her mother.

Dwelling on old emotional damage blocks us from becoming the spiritually-directed people we would like to be.

Liz was an only child. She grew up in a rural environment with few friends, had married unsuccessfully, divorced and had no children. Her career provided her with a central identity and much satisfaction, but she always felt something was missing and that she had not used her full potential. She had a lot of unresolved issues from her childhood with both of her parents, so there were cords dating back the entire forty years of her life. Some were quite healthy: cords of love, honoring and caring. Others were quite unhealthy, creating guilt and anger, which perhaps affected her relationships with her husband and her peers.

The current caregiving relationship was not successful, and in fact, was extremely painful for both Liz and her mother. They kept getting into situations that neither of them could back out of, saying things that neither of them meant to say and, in short, making each other totally miserable. Liz came to me to figure out how to do what she knew was right yet felt so wrong.

When I started working with Liz, I asked her, "I know you love your mother very much and she loves you, but do you think that removing some of the unhealthy connections of the past might help you to communicate better with her?" At first she was hesitant. Releasing the grips of old stories of her past that identified her seemed like losing something very essential. But with all that old business in the way, there was no room for growth and change.

We started removing cords. Some made her cry, some made her laugh. We kept many cords: the good shared experiences such as field trips, lovely picnics and walks—memories of times and feelings that were positive and kind. We removed the cords that were hurtful and unkind: misunderstandings, honest mistakes, errors in judgment, negative adolescent thoughts and fears. What was left was beautiful. Needless to say, once we had finished, Liz's relationship with her mother improved. As her mother's health gradually and gently declined, Liz continued to care for her and the situation moved through its normal process in a way that was healthy and life-affirming for both people. Within a few months, they were communicating in a way that neither had believed possible. It was a wonderful experience for all of us. What began as war, ended in peace.

DE-CORDING

Now that you have read this, you may be thinking, *Wow, I bet I have a ton of cords.* Well, you probably do, so let's take a look. It may seem a bit strange at first examining your energetic field for cords, but I promise if you give it a try, it is very easy. Don't worry whether it is your imagination or if it's real. The work is effective; it is real in a spiritual sense.

A good place to begin de-cording is the heart chakra. You can imagine that in your heart chakra you probably have chords to old lovers and friends, cords about sibling rivalries, etc.

Read through the exercise first to see how it works and then give it a try.

Get into a comfortable position, in a private place where you will not be interrupted.

Do a relaxation activity that works for you: breathing, yoga or meditation. Make yourself calm and make sure you have sufficient time to do the work, at least half an hour.

Close your eyes and visualize your heart, watch it beating and doing its terrific job of keeping you alive. Then look around it, notice places that feel tight or pulled. That is a good place to find cords.

Look for a cord and trace it with your mind to the other end. See who it attaches to. Quite often, the first cord you can find will be someone very significant in your life like a parent, spouse or sibling.

Make sure that you are picking an unhealthy cord; ask what this cord feels like. Does it feel like a healthy mutual flow of energy or does it feel like it binds you in some way that is not healthy or productive?

I'll give you an example of the process but work with the issue that arises for you. Suppose you're looking at a cord to your mother. You basically have a good relationship with your mom, but during adolescence you were really horrible and it made you both miserable. A lot of connections would still exist from that time but don't really apply to who you are now. It's a good time to remove the cords that are not useful.

It's helpful to visualize the cord and to whom it's connected, and then say, for example, aloud if you wish, "I am cutting this cord to you, Mom, because it represents a very negative connection between us. It represents my adolescent self, my embarrassment about it and my anger at your overbearing attitude at that time. I'm going to cut the cord and release this piece of our relationship."

If you don't feel comfortable using guides, you can cut the cord by yourself. Take the cord, cut it at your end and send it to any one of four places: air, earth, water or fire. If you send it to the air, towards the Light, that's the easiest place. It is sent to the universe to be transformed, as all energy and matter must be, into something better. If you send it to the water, it has a cleansing, washing away effect. If sent to the fire, it is consumed and purified. If you send it to the earth, it gets reabsorbed and becomes nutrient for something new to grow.

Once you have cut the cord, ask for healing light to come to the space. Imagine that healing light glowing on the place where the cord was attached (in this case, the heart), healing that spot. You might actually feel that something has been released from your body.

After you have cut the cord and enjoyed the release from that unhealthy tie, take another look around your heart for the next cord. It may be another cord to your mother, or perhaps to someone else. There may be ten or even twenty cords to significant people in your life. Several of them will be healthy ones; the remainder should probably be removed.

Once you have completed the heart chakra, move on to your throat chakra. As we have discussed earlier, the throat chakra often holds a lot of unexpressed emotion. There will be plenty of cords relating to self-expression. Continue with each of the chakras.

Maintenance

I recommend that this process be done at least annually, like any good housekeeping, as it is important to keep your energy body in good shape. Over time, you will get quite good at de-cording and come to really enjoy it. In fact, you will feel lighter each time you do it. It's rather like managing a forest by removing the unhealthy trees, leaving the trees that are healthy and vigorous enough space to grow, thrive and let in the light.

CHAPTER TEN

Meditation

Much has been written about meditation and I won't repeat the obvious here. The process is truly personal, so I will give you some ideas to start you on your way, but like everything about you, your meditation style is going to be your own. Finding the meditation practices that suit you is a worthwhile exploration that will reward you all your life.

I have been practicing meditation since the age of fourteen. It has gotten me through lots of tough times and helped to keep me from making many stupid mistakes born of anger or frustration. Just the process of stepping back and getting quiet has truly freed me in so many ways. When I was in graduate school, for example, I really wanted to go on a trip to the Grand Canyon that was going to be a lot of fun. But I knew that I had a dissertation to write, and this trip would severely hinder my ability to complete the task on time. My "fun" self said, *Oh you'll manage; it'll all get done.* But my serious self said, *No, you won't ever be able to make the trip* and *do all that work.* So I made a deal with myself: I would meditate and begin my work and if I completed half the work I needed to, I would go on the trip for a week. If not, I would remain home and stick to my books. It sounds like a simple solution. But by implementing a serious meditation practice, I was actually able to complete the work, all that was required and make the trip (I never made it to the Grand Canyon, but that's another story).

Beyond "Monkey Mind"

When beginning a meditation practice, you will invariably encounter the problem of quieting the mind. Indeed, the purpose of the practice is to interrupt the thought-forms of the conscious thinking mind so that deep calm and deeper listening and understanding become natural to you.

It requires practice to still the mind. It requires an emptying of all the thoughts that you usually are accustomed to that keep you company day and night, as though you have a friend who sits in your head and observes, chatters, comments and, in general, assesses what's going on around you. It's not a bad thing to have that voice assessing what's around you, but it does prevent you from allowing information to come in from the great unknown. Over time, you will gradually be able to quiet your internal dialogue and become freed of the constant mental chatter known as "monkey mind."

Why do we call it the monkey mind? Because unless the mind is calmed through practice, it leaps about like a monkey, aimlessly jumping from subject to subject, around and around. It is also described as one's "personal loop," which focuses on things that are negative or frustrating or things that we cannot complete. It can play in a continuous loop. For example, you may be thinking about the fact that you have a pile of laundry to do, that your car needs an oil change or that you need to decide what to have for dinner. Perhaps you are ruminating on all the errands you didn't get done today or who is going to win the baseball game or that you are too fat or that your car is in its last year. All of these things are stopping you from quieting your mind.

Unless the mind is calmed through practice, it leaps about like a monkey, aimlessly jumping from subject to subject.

Spend some time with your monkey mind. Become aware of its positive and negative aspects. It serves a valuable purpose, that of keeping you in this world and doing the things you need to do. In its best form, it is your reminder voice, your mom's voice, saying *brush your teeth, wash your face, remember to do the dishes.* But in its worst form, it is a constant loop of self-criticism, negation, nonsense and noise. It is a closed loop that can harm you, sometimes even torture you. Controlling the monkey mind is the key to meditation and in order to succeed at listening to the authentic voice of true wisdom, you must know this inauthentic voice first.

One thing I advise people to do, and what I do myself, is simply to make a list of all of these "monkey mind" topics. Then you can forget about them for the time being. You can put the list on your kitchen table and cross things off as you do them or just take a break from the remaining negative noise. It's the time and energy spent dwelling on these thoughts that's the problem, not the fact that we have them.

It is difficult to quiet the monkey mind, but there a lot of ways to tame it. Below you will find tips and exercises that are effective when practiced over time. In addition, you can listen to a meditation CD or download. You can make one yourself or you can buy any number of them. The most important thing when using recorded meditation is that you need to be sitting up because it's very easy to fall asleep when you're listening to them.

Some people go into the woods, a park or a deep forest. The calming sounds of nature often enable you to shut out all the other noise. You have to experiment and find out what works for you. You don't know what quiet is until you can still your mind. Once you've experienced your mind actually being still, it will be as calming as an effective drug. Over time, it will be a high that you can create without effort.

Yoga is another method of calming the mind through concentration that has multiple benefits. The original definition of *yoga* comes from the Sanskrit meaning union, connection, integration. From this philosophy grew the many disciplines of yoga, which are all intended to integrate body, mind and spirit. Currently there is a focus on physical yoga, which is intended to balance and move energy through the body. Many people experience the placing of one's body in different positions and holding them as a spiritual/meditative practice of its own. Physical yoga supports the practice of meditation, because when the body is flexible, strong and relaxed, the mind is free of thoughts about physical discomfort. You not only feel healthier; you are also able to meditate longer and with better focus. You may wish to locate a yoga class near you and try this balancing, strengthening technique.

Beginning Your Practice

I recommend committing fifteen minutes twice per day to meditate. It is often helpful to begin with five minutes and work your way up. More is better, but a daily commitment, however small, is more important than the length of time. All my beginning meditation students say they couldn't possibly sit still for that long, but after a few weeks, not only are they able to sit for fifteen to twenty minutes without any problem, but they also find that they feel refreshed and excited.

Using a timer is helpful. Many people who begin a meditation practice often find it difficult not to think about how long they have sat and how much time is left. Setting a timer allows you to relax and focus on your meditation by creating an end time.

A daily commitment to meditate, however small, is more important than the length of time.

Do not lie down. That probably should be the first rule of meditation: do not lie down! The reason is simple. Meditation is not sleep. It is a state of quiet mind but not a state of sleep. Sleep is not a quiet mind; sleep is a time for processing old business and new information. What we are trying to do in our meditation is still the mind. Or in the words of one of my favorite teachers, Swami Bharati: "Empty, empty, empty..."[6]

There is no one right way to meditate. But all meditation begins with the breath, *prana*. The word *prana* actually means life. We cannot live without breath and controlling our breath, just as athletes do, is essential. If you breathe too quickly when you go for a run, you will run out of breath before you get past the first block. The same is true of meditation. Controlling your breath controls the quality and depth of your meditation.

Let's revisit the breathing exercise we learned in Chapter Three. Then, I'll share with you some of my favorite forms of meditation. You can go on YouTube and look up over a thousand kinds of meditation. But let's start simply with the breath.

---

[6] Bharati, Swami Jnaneshvara. Yoga Nidra Meditation: Extreme Relaxation of Conscious Deep Sleep, Tranquility Press

MEDITATIONS: STILL THE MIND

BREATHING MEDITATION

Begin by assuming a comfortable sitting position in a quiet place, your sacred space or another suitable place at a time when you know you will not be interrupted. Wiggle around a little until you are really comfortable. Close your eyes.

Breathe in through your nose and out through your mouth. Let the in-breath be to the count of 4. Now breathe out through your mouth to the count of 8. (If that is too difficult, start with 2 counts in and 4 counts out.) IN 1-2-3-4 / OUT 1-2-3-4-5-6-7-8.

Practice this over time, increasing the count. A good goal is 16 in-breaths through your nose to 32 out-breaths through your mouth. If you are gasping, back it down. The idea is to slow down, not to breathe like you've run a mile. Do this for five minutes. It sounds easy, but it will take some time before you become competent.

As you breathe, rest your hands on your belly. Make sure that you feel your belly expand with the inhalation and deflate with the exhalation.

When you are counting, it is impossible to think of other things, therefore you are quieting your mind just by the very act of counting because you are too busy keeping track of the numbers. This circular breathing is a cornerstone of meditating.[7]

When you have mastered circular breathing, you can move on to a second type of meditation. You may find that the breathing meditation works just fine for you. It is in itself sufficient as a meditative practice, but let's try something else.

[7] Some wind musicians also use a technique called circular breathing, but that is a different method and purpose from the one we are learning here.

CHAKRA MEDITATION

In Chapter Three we discussed the chakras, so here I would just like to talk generally about chakra meditation. Our chakras, when clear, allow us to function optimally. Chakra meditation is a practice of going through each chakra and opening it up, fully cleaning it out, and allowing whatever energy is stuck there to flow out. It also allows whatever positive energy is around you to flow into the chakra. Often in chakra meditation, we visualize each chakra being filled with its appropriate color of light, a very nice feeling.

Chakra clearing is worth your time and attention. It is beneficial as a housecleaning function on a fairly regular basis, usually at least once a week. It becomes a sort of status update of places that might need work energetically or physically. For example, if you are feeling restricted in your throat chakra, you might want to send lots of sky blue light into that chakra and allow it to open up and let flow whatever is stuck there. It might be stuck because you have a cold, or because there are things that you need to say to someone. It's a good way to release that stuck energy.

The general process involves starting at the crown chakra and opening it up to the Divine Light. Each chakra in turn receives its appropriate color light and is opened and cleared. Try this practice regularly and the difference in your energy and your mental and emotional feel states.

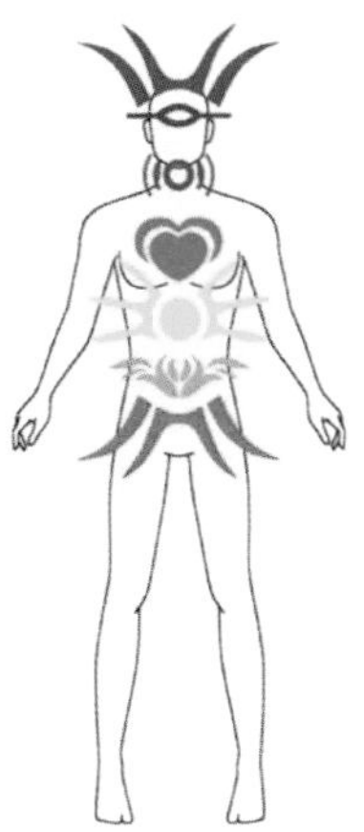

WALKING MEDITATION

Walking meditation is a centuries-old practice in many orders of monks. It is very good for people who have difficulty sitting still for a long time. Consciousness of your body and its movement is a living, breathing form of meditation, similar to yoga. It is also helpful when alternated with long sitting meditations; it's good to stretch your legs. Although it is a disciplined meditation, you can do walking meditation indoors or outdoors (as long as it is safe, because your awareness is drawn inward). It is the combination of motion and concentration on your physical action that allows you to do this meditation:

As you walk, completely focus on the movements of your body.

Do not pay attention to the surrounding area in which you are walking.

Totally inhabit your body, feel each muscle moving, feel your feet placing themselves on the ground, feel your breath moving in and out of your body.

I find this meditation almost impossible. I remember the first time I seriously tried to do a walking meditation. I was on an eleven-day silent retreat in Mount Madonna, California. It was a beautiful day. The jasmine was in bloom. Hawks were flying in the sky and the trees were enormous. I had never seen the giant Sequoia, and just the very feeling of them around me made me want to sit under them and look at them. Maybe if I was in a room that was boring and had no windows I could do walking meditation. I encourage you to try it, because it's a good idea to try all kinds of meditation. But, if you are easily distracted, it's probably not your best bet. I found it good to learn the discipline but it did not suit me. I am incapable of not smelling jasmine or looking at hawks.

In recent years, there's been a renewed interest in the labyrinth, a circular path that winds around upon itself. These circuits are ancient in origin and are intended for walking meditation. They are different from mazes, in that there is only one way in and one way out, so it's impossible to lose your way. Because your path is laid out for you, your mind is freed. You may want to find a labyrinth or create one in your garden or community. Churches, retreat centers and even some public gardens are good places to discover them.

GUIDED MEDITATION

Guided meditation is a way to communicate with your guides to learn different spiritual paths, and to gather information. Many recorded guided meditations for different purposes are available, but I want to discuss the kind that is usually done with a spiritual teacher. The teacher will talk you through a meditation process, allowing you to continue on your journey but remaining present to keep you safe and on your path.

The purpose of the guided meditation is always to learn something about yourself and your path. It allows you a safe way to walk in places that might be difficult to walk alone. I strongly recommend you begin with a teacher. If you don't begin with a teacher helping you, it is very easy to go to dark places. It's also easy to be confused by the information you receive, so it's good to have somebody to help you process it. For example, you may find yourself in a battle situation. Is this an actual battle? Or is it a metaphor, a particular feeling connected to a past or current incarnation? These things are important to understand, and it helps to have someone who has been on this path a number of times to work with you.

Your teacher will lead you through a simple relaxation technique. It can be a chakra meditation or just a way to release the tension in your body and quiet your mind. Then you will go on a spiritual journey, perhaps one in which you encounter your guides. It is often a place to learn a lot about yourself, your present life as well as your future and past lives. It is a doorway to your inner knowledge of yourself and also a doorway to the spirit world. Eventually, you will be able to do guided meditation on your own but it is always best to start with a teacher.

I worked with a young woman approximately thirty years old who had ALS, a severe life-threatening illness. She deeply felt that there were past life reasons for her illness and wanted to do a guided meditation called a "past life regression." We went on a journey and found that she had lived a long time ago in Italy. She had been a member of a small community that was persecuted for their belief system and was hiding people in a subterranean part of her villa. In this journey, all of the people in the villa were caught and killed by the Inquisition. Once we talked about the intense emotions of that experience, she was able to see the parallels to her current life challenges. She learned to contextualize them and as a result received some relief from her symptoms.

This is a pretty dramatic circumstance, and is only used as an example to give you an idea of the kind of things that can happen. Your guided meditation may be simpler. It may just be a way to figure out how to handle a situation that's posing you difficult problems at work.

I spent several years working with my teacher doing guided meditation at least once a week. I found that I was able to "house clean" a good number of my past issues from both previous life and present life and I was able to gain a clear understanding of what my path was to be as I continued forward.

You can use guided meditation to help you to make a decision. Call your guides in and ask them to work with you and help you to understand something that's confusing or difficult to decide. This process can be extremely rewarding and helpful. I encourage you to give it a try.

GROUP MEDITATION

Group meditation can be a truly wonderful experience. The energy of a large number of people all concentrating and listening to their breath can be very powerful. It is often done for long periods of time. I have sat in groups of more than one hundred people where every person in the room is meditating (well, maybe not every person, if you happen to fall asleep and snore). If you try a group meditation, you will feel the soul of the people around you, and it could create a nice feeling of solidarity and support.

Many practices have specific group meditations serving specific deities or purposes. They can be done in silence or as a guided meditation for the group. Just be aware that it can be confusing to sense others' emotions and feel other people's feelings if you don't have a well-defined boundary on your auric field.

What does that mean? It is not the same thing as creating a boundary to protect yourself by shielding; it is a little more open. What is often done when you sit in a large group meditation is that you create your "little home." You may choose to smudge your little area or bring sacred objects: a small statue, a special feather or rock, to bring your own personal energy to the space. Or, you may choose to lay out a blanket or pillows to delineate the space that you inhabit, even if it's only a four-foot by four-foot space. This allows you to keep your energy field clear when many things are going on around you. It is, however, a complex balance between keeping yourself separate to do your own work and allowing yourself to feel the buoyancy and support of others. I encourage you to try it at least a few times.

MEDITATING WITH SOUND

Some people find the slow, ambient sounds of New Age music very calming. Repetitive music is often used for counting; some find that classical baroque music can quiet the mind enough to meditate.

One person I know has a recorded heartbeat that he listens to. This sound calms him down and enables him to slow things to a pace where he can quiet his mind.

I recently began working with a man who uses binaural beats to do his meditation. He found a software application with different rhythms for relaxation, action, spirituality and many other purposes. It's similar to the function of drumming in meditation. As we have mentioned, many people find that using the drum, which replicates a heartbeat or similar body rhythm, allows their meditation to be more open. This can be done either in groups or alone.

Others choose to meditate to specific soundtracks, such as ocean waves, rain forest with bird calls, etc. Whatever calms your mind and allows you to become quiet works. Tuning into a sound pattern makes meditation easier for some people. If you do choose to use sound with your meditation, it's a good idea to use headphones so that you block out external noises. Try different patterns of sounds and see what might resonate with you.

MEDITATING WITH SIGHT, TOUCH AND SMELL

Some people use visual aids in meditation practice. One method is to stare at a pattern. Often something called a mandala is used; these are sacred geometric paintings, symbolic of the universe and have been used for centuries to create a focus point for meditation that helps quiet the mind. As you look at the mandala, you allow the beautiful patterns to draw you into the center. They enter your eyes and mind and quiet you. You might try using the mandala in the front of this book. Others may choose to look at a focus point or an image of the night sky. (I personally do a lot better with my eyes closed.)

You can involve your sense of touch in meditation. Think of the rosary or prayer beads. Touch provides you a way to stay on the course of your meditation practice by using the beads to count. Stones with different properties also provide tactile help for meditation.

Let's not forget the sense of smell. I am very fond of a particular smudge that is made of many lovely herbs. This smell alone can calm me down and quiet my mind. Try different scents and see how they affect you. Traditional smells that are associated with meditation are sage and lavender. You might explore aromatherapy and discover that certain scents affect your consciousness and inner vision in different ways.

I encourage you to play with all of these different methods and find what works for you. There is no right or wrong.

CHAPTER ELEVEN

Talking to the Divine: The Authentic Voice

Many of us have been brought up with the concept of prayer as integral to our evening activities, as part of our religious rituals or just a way to "petition the Lord." I believe prayer is much more than that; I believe we are all born with a direct channel to the Divine. Whether you define the Divine as the Source, the Universal Mind, the collective unconscious, God, the Void, or just the Spirit in the world, when you talk to Whomever that may be, that is prayer.

You should begin by thinking about the concept of prayer as establishing yourself in the space between heaven and earth. In the chapter about the chakras, we saw how the crown chakra focuses up toward the sky and the root chakra down into the earth. In order to pray, you must be grounded in the earth and you must open your crown chakra and your root chakra sufficiently to connect. Children know how to do this automatically, but often turn it off because adults are uncomfortable with the information their children receive—their "imaginary friends" or fantastic stories.

Let's take a moment to pray. Twenty minutes is a good time for this exercise. Give yourself the full twenty minutes, knowing that you need not be perfect at this practice in the beginning. Setting a timer, as we have discussed, will help you to relax and focus.

PRAYER

In order to be in balance, you need all your chakras to be open. Begin with your crown and move all the way down to your root chakra.

Allow your crown chakra to open, expanding from the size of a small knot to the size of a quarter, then to the size of a half dollar. Allow that opening to grow, expand and flower. As you bring your attention to this opening, it will naturally focus the Light that is around us all the time into that space.

Imagine a crown on your head that funnels the light into the chakra, allowing you direct contact with all that is divine, all that has come before us, all that will come after us, all that is in the world as we know it and even other worlds. Open yourself.

Move down to your third eye. Allow your mind to focus on opening and expanding its awareness to all that is around you, all that is seen and unseen.

Continue to your throat chakra. Feel the opening as you breathe and allow it to be as wide open as the sky. Feel the power of your voice.

Continue to your heart, the strong beating and the emotions of great knowledge and oneness with the universe. Feel the light moving down to your heart chakra, illuminating it.

Next open your diaphragm. Feel the light move down as you breathe slowly in and out.

Open your navel. Feel the seat of your connectedness to generations past and future.

Now move down to your root chakra. Feel your spine lengthen.

Feel the energy flow down through your legs to the earth. Imagine your feet growing roots that sink deep into the earth, reaching a place of warmth. Allow the warmth to flow up into your body.

Let the light from your crown flow down as the warmth from your root flows up. With each inward breath bring the light down. With each outward breath, bring the warmth up.

(continued)

Relax and do this exercise for a few minutes. Feel your place of balance between the earth and the sky. From that sacred space breathe deeply and quiet your mind.

Now ask a question that is important to you.

Often the question will be a simple one like "Will I meet someone who I will feel is a soul mate?" No question is foolish or invalid; all questions are good if you have genuine interest in knowing the answer. But realize that this is also an opportunity for you to receive information on a much greater scale, to download information from the universe. If you allow yourself to receive, you will receive much that is interesting. Continue this exercise:

Take deep calming breaths, inhaling for 4 counts/exhaling for 8.

As you finish these breaths, create the intention that any information that you receive will be to your greatest and highest good and to the universe's greatest and highest good. (I often add "to the benefit of all sentient beings," or "for the benefit of the earth." You can ask that it benefit your family and friends as well.)

Continue the breaths; allow your shoulders to drop and your body to relax. Then listen.

The Authentic Voice

As your meditation practice progresses and you begin to tap into your inner wisdom, you may find yourself wondering whether the voices you hear in your mind are your own inner dialog or divine guidance. This question is one of the hardest to answer, and something that I encounter with all of my students. Perhaps you have heard voices and are trying to sort out what they mean and where they originate. It can make you a little crazy not knowing where your thoughts begin and the "God voices" end. Sometimes I can't even tell. But I've learned the secret to figuring it out, and in this chapter I'll share with you the simple keys to discerning if it's just you or if it's an "authentic voice."

What is an authentic voice? When you are spoken to by the higher power of your own defining, that is an authentic voice. I often hear it when traveling in my car or doing the dishes, or just before sleep. A woman I work with calls such voices "highway angels" and says that they help her stay out of trouble while driving. They poke her if she's falling asleep. They tell her to take a turn to avoid a traffic accident, etc. I also have highway angels and I've mentioned my "parking karma" previously: no matter where I go, there is always a parking spot right in front of where I want to be. A voice says to me *Turn down this street right here and you will find a space.* Why doesn't this voice also tell me, for example, *Don't go out with that guy, he'll turn out to be a frog,* or, *You will look terrible in that dress?* But that's the point. We really can't control the voice; all we can do is learn to listen to it.

One of the things I've noticed about hearing voices is that often the people who are most likely to hear voices are the ones who are the most reluctant to hear them. Conversely, when someone comes to me and says "Please, I want to be psychic" or "I'd like to hear and channel voices," that often sets off an alarm for me. It is both naive and potentially dangerous to be so eager to acquire certain abilities that we ignore the training and seriousness which spiritual practice requires. Most of the folks that I work with in my shamanic practice are reluctant to hear voices. They question the authenticity of what they hear and quite honestly wonder whether or not they're crazy.

We really can't control the authentic voice; all we can do is learn to listen to it.

I have mentioned how lucky I was that no one in my family thought I was crazy when I heard voices or knew things that weren't ordinarily perceived. I certainly took my voices seriously (they were so frequent and accurate). As a kid, I hung out with a group that was a little rough around the edges. We did many things that I'm not prepared to talk about here. But one interesting thing always happened: if we were in a situation where trouble was impending, I would simply say to the group "It's time to get out of here," and because they implicitly trusted my "voice" (although that's probably not how they would describe it), we got out of there immediately. A bunch of teenagers were quite willing to accept that I was being guided by something, even if they didn't know what it was, and because it was dependable, they weren't taking any chances. We avoided many arrests and other unpleasant experiences!

You might ask why the voice would help me out when I was behaving so badly. Well, I think that God is pretty kind, and maybe She had some plan for me and wanted to keep me around long enough to do it. But again, the point is we can't control when we're spoken to. The only thing of importance is that we listen. Then, when we are actively seeking an answer to a question, we have prepared the way for divine guidance to enter and be heard.

Listening to the Voice: a Larger Perspective

In addition to being open to hearing the authentic voice, meditation is key to developing the ability to discern it. Let's take a look at a possible scenario that might arise in your practice.

Center yourself and begin the breathing exercise to quiet and calm your mind.

Open your chakras as in the exercise above, and ask God, Spirit, or your guides to give you the gift of hearing.

Once your mind is stilled, begin by asking a simple question, one which you know the answer to, such as, Should I give my child a nice birthday present? *Then listen.*

There's usually the voice that says things like: *Should I spend $100 or spend $50? He really likes that bicycle, but the budget's a little tight right now. Maybe I should just get the books*—and so on and so on.

As you probably have guessed, this voice is not your authentic voice but your monkey mind. In addition to "rigging" the answer to fit a desire, we may become stuck in a conversation that gets us nowhere.

I, too, can get into a bind with this issue. Say, for example, I want to spend some money on new shoes even though I really don't need them. So I think, *Well I'll still my mind and ask whether I should buy them.* (When you become a practitioner you try to integrate this practice into all of your decisions. Sometimes it can make you crazy.) So I still my mind and think, *Do I really need those expensive shoes?* My mind says, *Yes, you do, you'll feel so much better. You'll take longer walks, you'll exercise more, you'll be happy.* Then I still my mind further and it says, *No, you don't need them, you already have five pairs of similar shoes sitting in your closet. In fact, you should donate those shoes to charity because you hardly wear them.* Then I laugh at myself and think, *You are wasting all this divine time thinking about something that has no importance!*

More seriously, if someone seems dark to me yet I like them and want to spend time with them I may say, *Oh, I'm sure I'm wrong about them, you must be giving me someone else's messages.* You get the picture. We don't want to hear what we are being told because it doesn't fit what we think is our immediate need.

It might be something like shoes, or it might be whether to go out on that date with a particular person, or whether you should discipline your kids for something that they did yesterday. Although this behavior is never the best use of our meditation time, we are human and these issues inevitably come up. So how do I know if it's my authentic voice saying "yes shoes" or "no shoes?" The question is asked from a place of stillness, *but also from a larger perspective. This is the secret to hearing the authentic voice.*

By larger perspective I mean (using the shoes or birthday gift as examples) *asking the true and appropriate question such as "God, am I in a position to spend this money right now or do I need to be more frugal? Is this a genuine need?"*

The point of these examples is that we are human and tend to ask things and wish for answers that perhaps we ought not. Sometimes there are even dark voices that speak to us when we open our minds to the Light. So I would suggest not starting with questions that are going to impact your personal life in a small way, but rather questions that are larger and more meaningful. For example, you might ask the Divine in your meditation whether or not you should pursue a particular course of study, and whether this path would be of benefit to you and humanity. Perhaps you would ask, *Should I change my career and go into a helping profession?* Another important question might be, *Is there something I need to be doing for my child's illness that will help him heal more quickly?*

Make your mind as silent as you possibly can and listen. The voice may not be an actual voice for you. It may be an image or it may be tactile; you may need to touch your child in order to get the answer. We receive our guidance through many different means, but the first step is to be quiet enough to receive information about something where you have less of a "dog in the race," so to speak. That approach will help you to become freer in your decision-making process, and in listening to the voice.

Truth or Consequences

Now that we know what the inauthentic voice sounds like and how we may listen to the authentic voice, remember that it doesn't always tell you what you want to hear. My authentic voice has saved my life, but has also made me do a lot of things I didn't want to do. We may heed or ignore guidance. Here are two examples.

When I'm going on a trip, I ask whether the trip is safe and whether I should go. I ask about the things that I should do on the trip, including any work that I may be assigned by God. If I take a vacation, there is often something I have to do that's a trade-off. I'll give you an example.

Recently, I went on a trip to a Caribbean island with several close friends. Our hotel was very luxurious, the rooms beautifully appointed (our suite had three bathtubs). I had never stayed in such a luxurious place. But everywhere I went, even though I was surrounded by opulence, I felt the energy of voices that needed to be heard, voices of individuals who had died in slavery and needed to be crossed over to the other side. I thought, *Come on God, I'm on vacation, give me a break.* However, the price of admission for this trip clearly was that I do some work. I went out onto the fancy balcony, sat on the elegant chaise longue, and asked God what I was meant to do on this trip.

I was told in no uncertain terms that I was to listen to the voices of people who had lived in the place where I was currently resting my head on a very expensive bed and cross them over to the other side. I really wanted to just bask in the sun, swim in the pool and snorkel in the ocean. But I listened to my authentic voice telling me that I had work to do. So each evening at the end of an enjoyable day, I went back out onto the balcony and asked for specific instructions about what to do and how to do it. It may not have been the most fun vacation I've ever had in my life, but I listened to the voice of my master and heeded my guidance.

In contrast, you will recall my crossroads experience. I was the successful co-owner of a company which my partner and I had started from scratch and built into the largest company of its type in New England. My monkey mind was busy with financials, hiring and purchases. My authentic voice was equally busy telling me that something was very wrong. It was telling me that the time for me to be in this environment was over. I was meant to leave and do what I'm doing now: working with people to help them become their highest and their best selves through learning about their own spirituality, their own higher calling. But I didn't want to listen; I didn't want to be God's tool. I was pretty happy running a company that was "doing good and doing well," not to mention earning community accolades and a great salary.

When the authentic voice and your free will are in alignment, you are truly walking your spiritual path.

However, the universe had other ideas in store for me. And no matter how hard I fought it, or how many signs were given to me, or how loudly my authentic voice spoke to me, I didn't listen. Instead of walking out of a thriving business that would have allowed both business partners to succeed and move on to other things, I hung on to the bitter end. I fought change. I fought for control. Interestingly, my spiritual teacher repeatedly told me it was time to close down the business. He had heard in his guidance that I was meant to go on another path. I, in my ignorance, believed it to be his agenda, not his authentic voice. My ego got in the way of my ability to hear my voice, or to listen to his.

As a result, I suffered the loss of my business through a hostile takeover. I was left with a small child, a big house with a big mortgage and no income. Eventually, I set out on my current adventure, but I could have avoided a world of pain had I listened to my authentic voice.

The guidance that we receive is truly for our highest good. Now, over a decade down the road from this experience, I can see that it could not have turned out any other way. This is how it was meant to be.

Free Will and Divine Will

I think it's human nature to challenge the concept of something larger than ourselves. In some ways, it's a relief to believe that there's somebody calling the shots and in other ways, it's kind of frustrating to believe that we don't control our own destinies. This dovetails with the question of good and evil, and free will, which we will talk about in the next chapter. I struggled deeply with the experience of seeing terrible things happen and not being able to contextualize them. Why, if there were a God, would She allow a child to die, wars to occur or humans to be just so incredibly cruel to each other? Where I ultimately landed on the subject is that free will is the issue. We have free will so we can choose whether or not to do what is good and right. Every day with every decision we make, we use our free will to make choices that are towards the light or towards the darkness.

Often people who begin shamanic studies have a life-changing experience that brings them to me. Many of them have spent a great deal of time examining their belief systems and rejecting several others. Everyone is looking for something larger than themselves; I think it's just human nature. The folks that come to me are often in a place of great challenge. They often define themselves as agnostic: they are not sure that there is a God or that there is a higher power of any sort, but have seen evidence in some way that something divine has affected their lives. Perhaps you have had such an experience—this can be a small miracle of you or your child surviving illness or a more dramatic one like the gentleman we will meet in Chapter Fourteen who was cured of his cancer by divine light. Most people still question if there is something beyond what they can see, touch, hear, smell and taste.

So what does this have to do with voices? Allowing yourself to listen to the authentic voice allows you to align your free will with the voice of the Divine. That sounds complicated, you might say, but it is fairly simple. When you listen to your authentic voice, you will receive guidance about decisions. You will be protected in many cases from danger. But ultimately you have to make the choices about how you conduct your life. The real way lies in balancing: listening to the voices of the Divine and using your own free will. When the two are in alignment, you are truly walking your spiritual path.

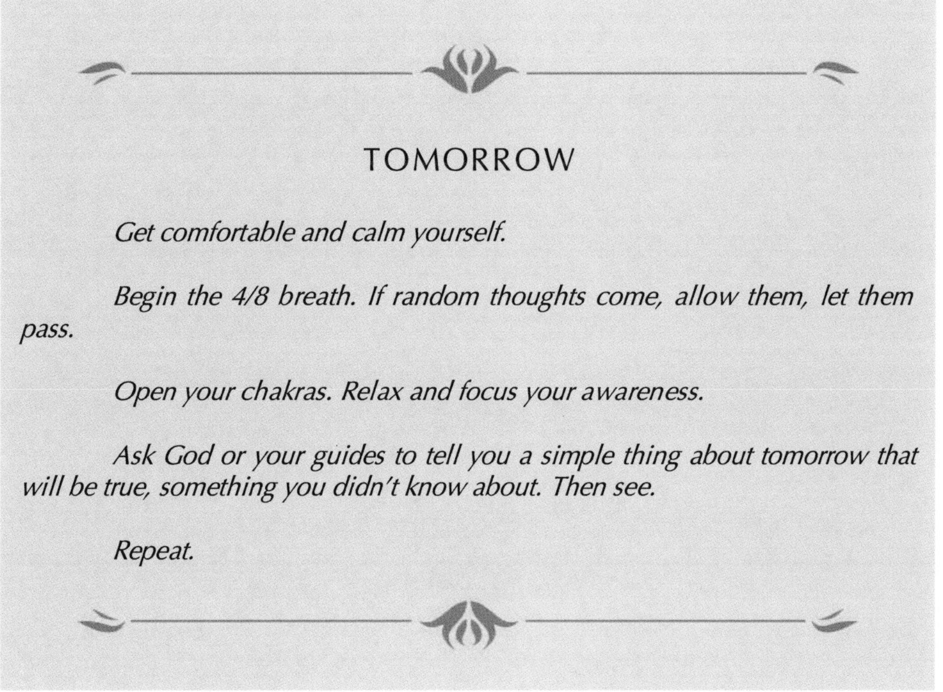

TOMORROW

Get comfortable and calm yourself.

Begin the 4/8 breath. If random thoughts come, allow them, let them pass.

Open your chakras. Relax and focus your awareness.

Ask God or your guides to tell you a simple thing about tomorrow that will be true, something you didn't know about. Then see.

Repeat.

How about asking what you should be doing to heal the planet? I believe that there are sources in the universe that wish us to survive and become a species in harmony with our environment. In order to do so, we will have to change our ways, every one of us. If we wait for the government (any government) to do it, it may never happen.

I would suggest that a good step in learning to listen for the authentic voice is to ask for a task that you can do as an individual to assist in this age of our planet. It might be helping at an animal shelter, or cleaning up your act about recycling and sustainability or whatever feels right to you. This approach, one that is for the good of others, will be a place where you are more likely to hear your authentic voice.

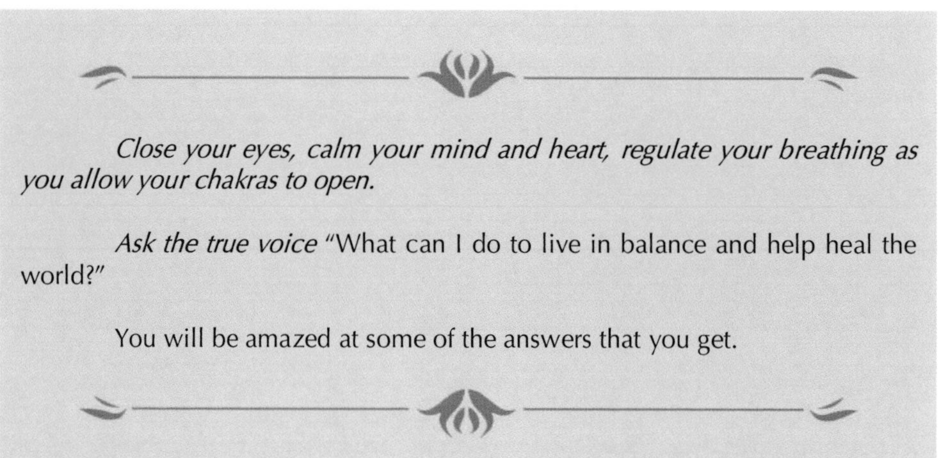

Close your eyes, calm your mind and heart, regulate your breathing as you allow your chakras to open.

Ask the true voice "What can I do to live in balance and help heal the world?"

You will be amazed at some of the answers that you get.

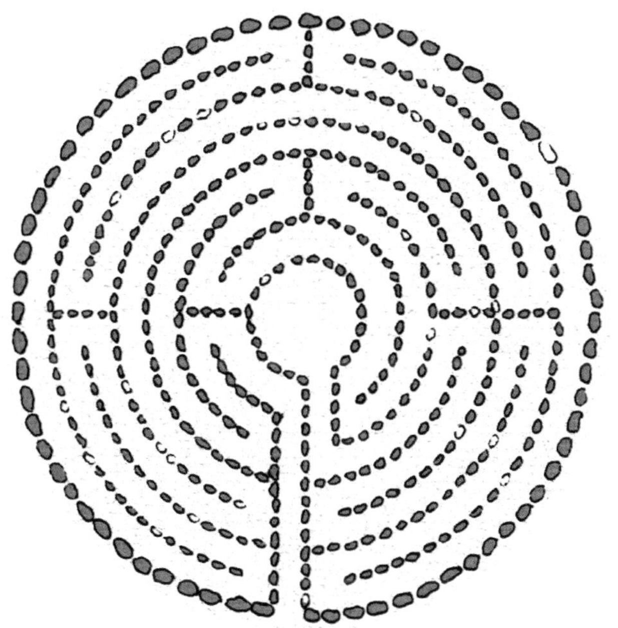

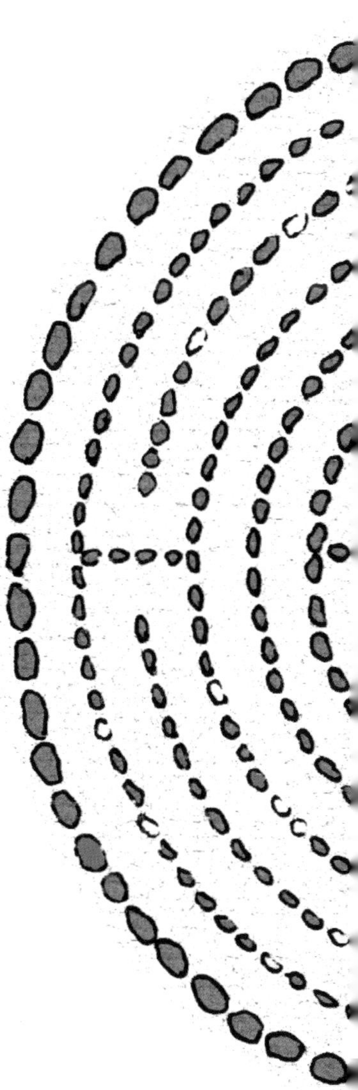

PART THREE

Life in the Balance

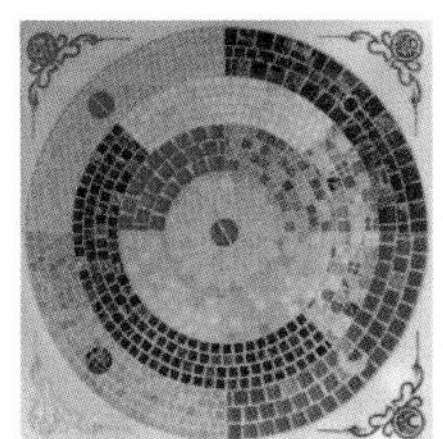

CHAPTER TWELVE

Good and Evil, Darkness and Light

People often ask me if I believe good and evil exist. Yes, I do. Whether you want to call them darkness and light or our shadow side and our better nature, there is, in fact, a real choice between what is right and what is wrong. There are, of course, shades of gray in life, something I had a difficult time understanding until I was a mature adult, but in matters of importance—make no mistake, good and evil exist.

I will try to do what philosophers have done for thousands of years; that is, come up with a working description of good and evil, one that will be useful and maybe make things a bit clearer for you. When I was a fledgling therapist, I really wanted to believe that everyone could be sorted out somehow; that regardless of the depth of the illness, the extent of the injury or the bad intention of those surrounding a person, with a lot of love and a little help, everything could be overcome and people could get well. I still believe we should act as if that is the case, but in the half-century of my life, I have seen so much darkness and bad intent that I can no longer accept that everyone and everything can be fixed. People who have suffered enormous abuse or neglect were treated in an evil manner. Even if no harm was intended, the actions themselves contained evil content, darkness.

It is incumbent upon all of us to try to mitigate, repair and in all ways counter these damaging effects, whether we do that in spiritual studies or just as neighbors doing the right thing, because ignoring obvious acts of darkness makes us complicit. If you see your neighbor beating his child and you don't report it, you are supporting evil. The neighbor's action is evil even if he's not evil himself. If you turned a blind eye on a dog tied up all day and neglected, you are supporting evil. If you believe that it's somebody else's problem, you are supporting evil.

So where does evil come from? For that matter where does good come from? Perhaps the clearest way of thinking about evil is to come up with a definition of good to create the contrast. Any definition of good must include the concept of "the Source," the place where we all began, the Big Bang if you will, or the first day of Creation, whatever feels like "The Beginning" to you. Whatever it was that intended for the creation to emanate and evolve we can call the Source, or God, or, if you're in the right mood, the collective unconscious. It's is the repository of all that is good, all that is right.

Happiness is, by its very definition, good. If you are in a state of joy or bliss, there is no room in your heart for evil. Think about it: can you have bad, resentful, or angry thoughts about a person when you're happy? Can you hold happiness and anger at the same time? I don't think so. If you feel you can, perhaps that thought is itself evil. So happiness, light, goodness and joy create a space that is positive. On the other hand, of course, resentment, anger, bitterness, fear and anxiety can create darkness; not always, but they allow the space for it to enter. So if you are looking to exclude evil in your life, simply be happy all the time. We all hear talk of creating a positive space or not leaving room for sickness and darkness. But easier said than done...and what does that mean experientially? Can we really control our thoughts and actions?

In an Eastern view of the world, the Source comes from above our crown chakra and enters our body, filling us with "God light." This light is good; it feeds us. It is that which creates and brings us into being. It is the spark of life. What could be better? Another way of framing it might be to say that anything that brings joy and contentment, happiness and giving, caring and healing is by its very nature the source of good.

So then what is evil? Is it just the absence of good? I don't think so. I think it is a force in its own right. I believe that we can recognize evil. If you have an animal living in your space you are blessed in many ways, one of which is that they are great detectors of intent. When I was a child, we raised and showed German Shepherds. They are very intelligent dogs. My favorite shepherd was a dog named Stormy. He was not the most beautiful dog in the world, but he had an amazing sense of wrong and right, good and evil. I remember taking him for walks often and being surprised at his reactions to various things. (As children we are often quite innocent and do not see dark intent.)

One night on a walk with Stormy, I met a man who I had seen behind the counter at a deli where I loved to go and pick sour pickles out of a barrel. This man seemed overly friendly to me as we met that evening on the street, but as he was not really a stranger, I felt okay talking to him. After a minute or two, he asked if I was alone, and if my parents were home. I got a bit concerned, but when Stormy gave me a signal of a low growl, I decided to run. As we sped down the street, I felt a bit foolish and even rude. But my wonderful dog had sensed the intent of this man as a predator. Later I found out that he had kidnapped a young girl in the neighborhood.

Stormy's sense of good and evil was innate. We can and should build that quality into ourselves. Here is a place where the "authentic voice" we spoke about comes in. I invite you to think about times when someone just didn't "feel quite right," or a situation felt dangerous or your reaction seemed unusual. Listen to that voice. Does it really matter if that man had a bad childhood? Perhaps to those entrusted to help him, but not to those who could be harmed. We ignore our evil sensors at our peril.

I have always found one of the strongest symbols to be the yin/yang symbol. It is half black and half white, but in the center of each is the opposite color, and it is forever circling itself, ever creating a dynamic sense of balance between the dark and the light, between good and evil. Perhaps we only see good because there is evil. Perhaps we only see evil because there is good. Just as healing is inherently good, harming is inherently evil. There are, of course, situations where we cause harm such as defending our loved ones or others in a dangerous situation. We could endlessly discuss the morality, the good or evil question in regards to war, uprisings or protest. But that type of experience is not something that most of us encounter in our daily life; the choices in our daily life are more personal and individual.

When I was just beginning my healing work, my teacher, a strong and powerful shaman, spent hours trying to convince me that there were no such things as good and evil. I strongly disagreed with him. I have faced evil. I know that it is real. He believes there is only illness and wellness, that people can be healed and that there really is no inherent evil, although he does believe in darkness despite the fact that he himself has struggled against evil, fighting darkness, and working with powers that are intimidatingly strong for most of his adult life. What I didn't understand in that moment, and what would, in fact, take me years to understand, is that however we frame things, there are clear lines that need to be drawn. There are things in which there are no gray areas and those things should be understood and taken seriously.

I have seen evil. I think we all have. There are some actions that have no other context possible, such as the random taking of another life, the injuring of a child, the harming of an innocent animal. These things are clearly wrong.

When I talk to people about evil, I am often given the argument that the offenders had a bad childhood, they were misunderstood, other kids made fun of them or they lived on the wrong side of the tracks. Yet I have seen some people overcome incredible obstacles, create awe-inspiring works of art or otherwise bring beauty into this world when all they were offered by life was darkness. Evil is a choice. It is possible to do evil things without consciousness but that does not make them less evil. We have to walk the world with intentionality or life has no meaning at all. Of course, sometimes harm occurs that is unintentional: we accidentally injure someone, or our car spins out of control and hits a deer and so on. These are not acts that are done with intention, therefore they are not evil. I would even argue that the person who loses his mind and injures many people and then kills himself may not inherently be evil. He may be very ill and confused. It all has to do with intention.

I spent four months of precious time working with my teacher stuck on this question: "If I could heal, does that mean I could unintentionally do harm?" His answer was always, "Yes, but you wouldn't." For some reason I couldn't accept that answer. It bothered me. I didn't want this power; I didn't want this feeling that somehow there was a strength in me that could do others harm. To that statement he always wisely answered, "You could go to a gun store and pick up a gun and kill someone with that." That choice exists for every one of us every day of our lives. After all, there are much more simple ways to harm someone than to put all your energy into using your mind, your power and your look and directing your life force to harm.

No matter how much my teacher argued with me, and he did argue with me, I still didn't want this power. Even if I didn't use it, I didn't want it. I found it very difficult to tolerate the thought that in a moment of weakness my intention could actually do harm. But I would not. As a conscious human being working to create Light, I work each day to create space for Light to come in. It is all about our intent. When we "walk the beauty way," as Navajo philosophy sees it, we are striving to live in balance with all things, to do no harm and to create space for Light at all times.

Intention is Key

We talked about intention earlier. I often say to people in my work that there are no ends, only means. In other words, as soon as we attain a goal of any sort, as soon as we achieve our end, we create another goal. This process constantly keeps us in a state of moving the horizon forward, thereby never achieving our end goal. It can be a wonderful thing, keeping us current, alive and active or it can be frustrating, making us feel that we never get to where we are aiming. If we reframe the subject by saying that there is no end, only the process by which we get there, it allows us to live each day, each minute, as an individual unit and stay in the present. This is something that all Eastern philosophies ask us to do: stay in the moment. Staying in the moment with the consciousness of creating Light and doing good is the essence of a spiritual path. It is becoming a conscious being and leaving no space for evil. With the clear intent and "awake" activity of the mind, we become a force for good.

I realize now that the argument I had both with my teacher and with myself was more about understanding that there is darkness in me, as there is in everyone. Every day we all make a choice about how to conduct ourselves in the world, whether or not to use our energy to do good or to do harm, even in the simplest of things like recycling or being kind to strangers. But it is within such small acts, make no mistake about it, that the shadow side or darkness can also reside.

As you begin this walk, the spiritual path, you are taking responsibility not only for your acts and your intention, but for the intention of those whom you teach, those who depend on you, and those you just meet on the street. I think that's a good thing. Acting with intention is being truly conscious.

CHAPTER THIRTEEN

Life Force

In order to understand the concept of who we are and how we exist within the framework of the universe, we need to talk about life force. Life force has many names. It is something that is recognized in all cultures, where it may be called *chi* or *prana*. The Chinese longevity god is represented with his upright body, and the flame that he holds in his hands is the strong life force that allows one to live to a healthy old age. Life force is the essence of our being, something that is difficult to describe with colors or words. It is an essence much like an aroma that you sense and know exists but cannot put your finger on easily.

Simply put, the life force is our will to live on a spiritual, emotional and biological level. It's what keeps us fighting to stay alive. When it is our time to go, our life force fades. I'm sure some of you have seen this when a relative becomes critically ill and dies. One moment they are present as the person you know and then it seems in an instant that something is missing, something that feels like the essential piece of who they are. They may still be breathing, their body may shut down sometime after, but some essential part of them is gone. We know when the lights dim and fade and then go out. What is missing is their life force. Their soul has gone (perhaps to enter as a new person and a new lifetime, but that's a story for another discussion).

Life force came up as an interesting conversation recently. I was talking with a young woman of twenty who is going through a lot of physical and emotional difficulties. She has suffered enormously with problems of autoimmune disease and drug withdrawal. I reassured her and said that she had many bountiful years ahead of her. She asked me, "How do you know that I'm going to get well?" My answer to her was, "Because you have a very strong life force." She asked me what a life force was and I realized it was hard for me to explain. I tried to put it the simplest way I could, and said to her, "You know how someone with very challenging physical problems can live a long time, be active and live their life to the fullest?" Then I told her about one of my personal heroes.

A True Hero

Matt is a wonderful gentleman who had been born with a rare neurodegenerative disease. Despite the fact that he came from a difficult family background, he managed to complete college and graduate school, and attain a significant position in a large company. He also found a wonderful woman to love and marry.

Matt is the least bitter human I have ever met. He is very active on the board of the disease association that represents his illness. He speaks regularly to large groups, tirelessly raises money for research, and each day he still hopes that there will be a cure.

I know from talking to him, from his medical information and from being an empath that he is in considerable pain every day, even on his pain medication. Yet I have never heard him complain. Most amazingly, I always hear of him talking about the future and what he can do for people with similar problems, including the children that will be coming up with these challenges, how they will find work and conduct their lives. He talks about how blessed he is. This person has an amazing life force in a very difficult life.

When I think about the concept of life force, I remember how much I really like to talk to nurses. They are the front line in any hospital. They are the ones who really know the details about what a patient is experiencing and have the medical knowledge to contextualize it. Over the years, I have asked nurses why, with the same set of circumstances, some people live and some people die and I have gotten enormously divergent answers. But the one thing most of them say to me is that the ones who live have that light in their eyes. Matt is such a life force.

Karma: The Big Question

The concept of karma in regard to life force is an interesting one. I have spent many, many hours thinking about this topic. All too often in my practice, women ask me questions such as "What have I done in my life to cause my breast cancer?" The question makes me want to cry. Did they do something in this life to cause the problem? Is there a reason they are in this situation? Do I even want to think about making that kind of judgment? I do not. I don't know the answer but I live with the question constantly in my work.

What do you think? Are we born with a certain length of time to live, and when "the meter runs out" do we simply end? If we are given a life force from the beginning, how much control do we really have over what happens in our lives? Do we ask for illnesses or challenges in life, or for that matter, do we ask for the parents that we receive? Many great thinkers who spend their time pondering these matters feel that we do. I'm not so sure that it is possible to know the answers, but what I do know is that the "blame and shame game" is useless and destructive.

The blame and shame game is played by many folks, and often by family members. It goes like this: "If only I had not smoked in college I would not have asthma now." Well, maybe and maybe not. There may have been a chakra disturbance that felt calmed by smoking (not that I in any way advocate doing so), and you, at that maturity level, felt better doing so. Or you may not have been strong enough to fight peer pressure. In order to heal and to sustain a good healthy life force, it's essential to remove this dynamic from your life. People with a healthy life force do not dwell on the past events or circumstances that may have brought them to their current status. Sustaining a strong life force requires living in the present.

This subject often gets personal for me. One of my dearest friends is currently at the end stages of her cancer, having been diagnosed only a few short months ago. I asked her how she felt and she said, "I'm really angry at my body. I eat properly, don't drink to excess, exercise, take supplements and do everything right. So why did my body betray me?" I told her, of course, that being angry seemed to me like a pretty natural response, but one thing I must say about this wonderful, loving, beautiful person who has dedicated her life to helping others is that she never really felt to me like she had a very strong life force. There was always a quality of sadness and a lack of joy in her daily life. She was always looking at the glass as half empty. I wonder, did this influence her ability to fight what has come to be understood as a genetic disease? Would having a stronger life force have affected the course of events? I have no answers, only questions. She also was living in great blame and shame, ashamed she could not cure herself and blaming external events for her plight. Of course, we should limit our exposure to things that are harmful to us, but to internalize it as blame or shame is self-destructive.

Affirming Life

So how can we foster our life force? It's simple but does require effort, focus and determination. As we have mentioned, the discipline that is required is primarily that of learning how to be present. Very little is gained by thinking *If I had salted the steps I would not have fallen and broken my leg.* You will probably not die from a broken leg, but you learn that the next time, it's important to salt the steps. We learn these lessons every day. They may not be as obvious as a broken leg, but they can be just as painful.

> The balance of life-affirming actions for ourselves and others helps us to be strong in our life force.

If you are in your "monkey mind" all the time you are never present. You are never enjoying your life. You are therefore not nurturing your life force. Of course it's important to go to the gym, eat properly, and do all the things that are required for your health, but nurturing your life force requires a self-awareness of when you feel strong and when you feel weak. One of the simplest things that foster your life force is allowing yourself to rest when you are tired, to say no to your friends when they want to go out and do something fun but the best thing for you to do might be to stay home and read a book.

One thing that drains your life force is spending a lot of time focusing on things that you have no control over. A very smart woman that I know once said "The most important thing is to figure out who's problem it is; it probably isn't yours." To learn what is your "portion" is very crucial. I listen to the news, but I am careful not to absorb pain that I am unable to do anything about. We all hear stories about compassionate people who die an early death. In part, it's because they have absorbed too much of the negative energy and pain around them. We can be aware of the events of the world, be aware of the pain, and do what we can within the context of our life to alleviate suffering, but we should not absorb it into our being.

When I worked in geriatric care I used to say jokingly that the people who live the longest are those who are completely self-involved. There may be some truth to that extreme statement. These people never worried about anything at all. They were careful about their comfort, often at the expense of others, but nonetheless they focused on living in a way that few do. I'm certainly not advocating total focus on oneself and one's needs to the exclusion of others, but what we can learn from these people is that focusing on oneself in a balanced way and knowing what we are capable of changing keeps us strong and alive.

Conversely, doing good deeds helps support our life force. These actions are positive and support both our emotional self and others: volunteering at a shelter, sending money to people who are less fortunate than we are or just making up a donation bag regularly and getting it to the correct place. These things nurture the goodness in ourselves but do not reduce our life force. They support it. It is this balance of life-affirming actions for ourselves and others that helps us to be strong in our life force.

What does someone's life force look like? It actually looks and feels like a living, vibrating thing. Auras, as you remember, are the lights that shine around someone's energy body. How they look and their colors tell you a lot about a person's state of being and health. Because I believe that we all have some innate intuitive abilities, I have taught programs for various groups about becoming your own intuitive. On the next page is a fun exercise from one of my classes that you might want to try.

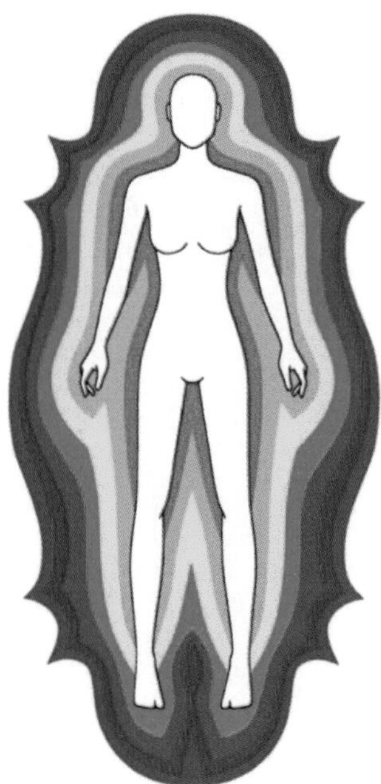

DRAWING THE LIFE FORCE

Get a box of crayons, one of the big ones with all the great colors in them and sit across from a friend. (Unfortunately, just like childhood you will have to share the box).

Draw the person's body. It doesn't matter whether or not you are able to draw; if you must, just draw circles for the head and body.

Then put in the chakras.

Draw the aura, the egg-shaped circle around their body.

Now close your eyes, allowing your mind to relax and your inner vision to take over.

Put the colors that you see for each of the chakras in and around the energy body. Let your intuition choose the colors, whatever they may be.

When you have finished, look at your drawing. If the colors are strong and bright and if they seem to shine from that person, that person has a strong life force. If you see dark spots or muddy colors, that is not a good sign. Keep in mind, however, that this is a picture of the person at this moment, and not a permanent energy portrait. Tomorrow those colors might be gone; your friend may have had a cold or virus or just been in a funky mood.

Once you have drawn this picture of your friend, it's also fun to draw one of yourself.

Two Forces

Two examples from my own life really brought the concept of life force home for me. They are my mother and my daughter, the female bookends of my life, if you will. They showed me that life force is indeed a significant factor in people's survival and thriving.

My mother, who is in her late eighties, still seems like the "Energizer Bunny." Ironically, she was always the sick one of three siblings; she suffered from asthma and related respiratory complaints all of her life. She never exercised a day in her life (her sport was shopping). Her four food groups are chocolate, coffee, cream, and butter. As a small child, she had rheumatoid arthritis and was bedridden for more than a year, which damaged her heart and raised the question of whether she would be able to live a normal life, let alone bear and raise children. She was always anemic, sickly and small for her age and considered frail by her entire family.

By contrast, her brother was a strong burly man who served in the armed forces and played baseball. The story in my family is that had he not been drafted into the Army, he would have played professionally. He died at eighty, still a ripe age, but he was ill for many years before his death and had a very low quality of life from age sixty on. Mom's sister was considered a health food nut: she ate healthy food, never smoked, drank lightly and led a pretty peaceful life. She died in her sixties of colon cancer.

The remaining survivor of this family is my mother, the one who was always ill. What did she have that they didn't have? An incredibly strong will to live. She wanted to be alive and still does every day of her life. She has survived things that many people would not, both physically and emotionally, and here she stands, strong, healthy and mentally intact. Now *that* is a life force.

When my daughter was born, it was doubtful whether or not she and I would make it. We had both contracted severe infections in the hospital. The pediatrician came to me the morning after her birth and said, "I've seen a lot of babies in the last thirty years and I know that this one will live." He meant that he could see her life force, her strong will to survive radiating from her tiny body.

The Present is a Gift

It always amazes me that life force has so little to do with physical condition or even emotional condition. It has nothing to do with whether someone exercises or takes good care of themselves. We all know the smoker that lived well into his or her nineties, and the fifty-year-old who never smoked but died of lung cancer. You can build your life force; you can nurture it with disciplined meditation exercises and healthful life practices. But you cannot create it.

I'm not trying to depress you, nor do I recommend smoking, drinking or other harmful things you might want to do! Those things will have detrimental effects on your health and can certainly curtail your time on planet Earth. But my point is that there are some things that are simply out of our control. People seem to expect that they'll live forever. It seems to be something that we "boomers" brought into being because there are so many of us. It's almost an entitlement to live a healthy life, as if disease were not a normal part of aging. Many of us are blessed with enormous life force. You've seen these people; they are often referred to as "live wires." These people seem to draw their life force from the very air that they breathe, and, in fact they do. You can too, if you stay present, as we will discuss in the chapter on living in the present moment.

Life force can glow from the eyes of someone eight or eighty. Although you may not be able to know exactly what life force you were born with, the truth remains that the best way to expand the quality and the quantity of your life and enjoy the time that is given to you is still eating the right foods, exercising, meditation, prayer and surrender.

CHAPTER FOURTEEN

Miracles

Anthony is a man in his early forties who was diagnosed with a cancer in his lung. He'd never been a smoker, his parents hadn't smoked when he was growing up, nor did he work in an environment where there were a lot of smokers. He was shocked, dismayed and confused. He and his wife have a very young child who he would like to see grow into a woman. There was little chance that it was not cancer; the oncologist had said that the particular signature of the tumor growth that they saw often indicated a cancer.

He came to me because the night before he was going to have a second CAT scan prior to surgery to biopsy the cancer, he had a dream. In this dream, which he calls a "lucid dream," he was in his bed with his wife, then got up and walked right through the window of his bedroom. The sky was cloudy above him. He thought, *It would be nice to see some sunlight.* Suddenly, the clouds parted and a ray of light illuminated his body below his shoulder.

The next day, he went in for the CAT scan, and the cancer had completely disappeared. Anthony, a lapsed Catholic, declared agnostic and "possible atheist," came to me because he felt that there must be a reason for this occurrence; there must be a reason he was spared. The doctors called it spontaneous remission. I call it a miracle.

I've heard it said that a miracle is any unexplained circumstance that comes out the way we want it to. Perhaps, but I have seen many miracles in the course of my work and these miracles seem to me to be an intervention, a sparing of someone. Why would someone be spared? I often meet with people who feel that they have been chosen. It is as if a light bulb has gone on over their heads showing them that there is more than what they see in their familiar lives. This circumstance can be something that they wished for and always wanted or it can be something quite difficult for them to accept. They may feel that their lives were in order and now, all of a sudden, they are not in order anymore. They have questions they never had before. Their previously easy dismissal of religious beliefs is gone and they wonder why things are the way they are. These people are often open for miracles to occur.

A miracle can be very small or very large. If you are reading this book, you are probably wondering if you have a higher path and if miracles can happen to you. I would very strongly say, *Yes, you do have a higher path and miracles can happen to you.*

Within the same week of meeting Anthony, I found out that my dear friend, who I have talked about earlier, had a very aggressive form of stage IV metastasized lung cancer. Celine is a woman who has dedicated her life to helping other people. She's a nurse, has never smoked, drinks moderately, eats properly and exercises at least three times a week. She was treated aggressively with chemotherapy, to no avail, and within a few months she had entered hospice care. She is furious that her body has betrayed her. At this writing she is fifty-two years old.

The juxtaposition of these two people, one who was spared and clearly asked to serve (more on that later), and one who has served all of her life, is difficult for me to understand or even comprehend. Why does one person merit a miracle and another a rapid decline in a few months? If you think I have the answer, you are sadly mistaken. But I do believe that there is a choosing that occurs. Possibly you are reading this book because you have had your own small miracles. You may have experienced events that intrigued you, perhaps made you wonder why you are alive and other people are not.

We pray for miracles. We cry out for miracles. But I think they simply occur when they are meant to occur, by some intelligence that we can't possibly know. I do know, however, that all of the people that I have worked with who have been spared in a way that might appear miraculous, have had much to do in this world. Their work always involved making the world a better place either by healing the environment or healing others. We might question who receives a miracle or even what constitutes a miracle. But can we doubt that they exist?

Look for the ways you are talented, gifted, strong, interesting, kind and loving—and allow yourself to think of them as miraculous gifts from the Universe.

I have been lucky enough to be part of some small and some larger miracles. I am able to be a channel by which people are healed. Sometimes, I can lay my hands on someone and feel whatever is wrong with them melt away. Sometimes it's a tumor, sometimes it's anxiety and sometimes it's an ulcer or a gallstone. I can't take the credit for these miracles. Something is acting through me and I take that very seriously, never for granted. I always know that it isn't me bringing about the miracle, but something working through me. And I am honored to be so served and serving.

The concept of miracles has been around for as long as people have existed, and appears in all religious belief systems. As a spiritual counselor, I could give you hundreds of examples just from my own experience, but I'm sure you've had your miracles too. We wonder: What constitutes a miracle? Does it have to be something large and imposing? Remember my "highway angels?" I am often told when I'm driving to go a different route, even if it's less convenient. Often this is because something has happened that would have caused me to be injured or delayed for a long time. Do you consider this a miracle? Whatever you call these occurrences, they are unexplainable, and thereby miraculous by their very nature.

You may or may not believe that Jesus rose again. You may or may not believe that Moses parted the Red Sea. It doesn't really matter. If you look for miracles in your everyday life you will find them. Isn't it miraculous that you just get up every morning and your body works in harmony? Isn't it miraculous that we can bear children and watch them grow up? I ask you to look at your life and examine the kindnesses and good experiences that you've had and wonder if they have not been given to you as a gift. Perhaps a better description for miracle might be something beautiful that we absolutely did not expect to happen, yet it did. And isn't that a wonderful way to be in the world?

Can we encourage miracles? I think we can. I think we can be open to the possibility that the world is greater than our sensory experience and by that I mean our experience of our traditional five senses. We hear, but to be transformed by music is a miracle. We see, but to be moved by a piece of artwork is in its own way a miracle as well. If we look for them they are all around us. Isn't it a miracle just to breathe?

We spend an awful lot of energy thinking about the things that are not right in our lives. I encourage you to spend some time thinking of the small and great miracles in your life. I try to remember to pray every night. The first part of my prayer is always *Thank you, God, for all the gifts that you have chosen to give me.* I think that being who I am is a miracle. I did not ask to be who and what I am, yet this great gift was given to me. I try never to take it for granted. I would ask you to do the same: look for the ways you are talented, gifted, strong, interesting, kind and loving—and allow yourself to think of them as miraculous gifts from the Universe.

PART FOUR

Being Human

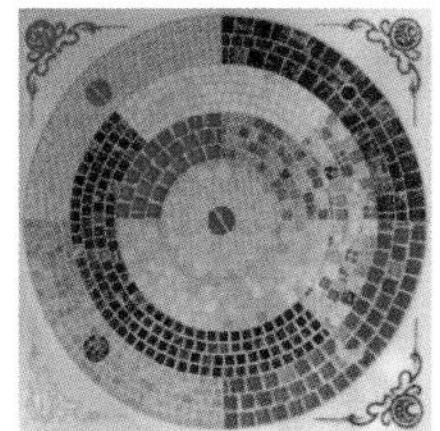

CHAPTER FIFTEEN

Negative Emotions

Grief and Loss

As with most people, I find loss much easier to deal with in the abstract and much harder when it is personal. I have mentioned that I am dealing with the loss of a very close friend. She is very ill and soon will be leaving this dimension. I would like to tell you that I approach her death with equanimity, that I am calm and sure that she will be happy on another plane. But I find, like everyone else, some of life's trials much more difficult than others. It's hard to be calm at the prospect of the death of a child or someone who is in the prime of her life. Where are the words to make us feel better about grief and loss?

I feel that in our current culture there is not enough latitude given for the process of actual mourning. In the Victorian era, when people lost a loved one, the colors they wore and the length of time they wore each color were formally prescribed. Initially, they wore black, then purples, grays and after a time they could wear more variety of colors. Everyone knew from their attire where they were in the process of mourning. This may have been a rather rigid way of dealing with the situation, but in some ways it was a lot easier. Nowadays we are expected to pick ourselves up after a significant loss and just keep going.

Grieving and mourning are not something to be ashamed of, but something to be embraced. Loss and death are part of life and if we repress this part of our emotional expression because it is embarrassing or we live in a culture that denies it, we are denying a huge part of our humanity. In a perfect world, we would come to a place of acceptance. We would understand that everything that is born lives and dies, and perhaps is born again.

Several years ago, I lost my father and my brother within a month of each other. I tried very hard to approach their deaths from a place of acceptance, as a natural transition, and I think that for the most part I did. But once their passing and the funerals were over, it was difficult for me, and my memory of that time is basically a haze of numbness and pain. I don't think that I was angry or even felt grief; I was just confused and dazed by the fact that I was getting a one-two punch and had to find a way to stay on my feet during it.

One of the things I chose to do during this time of loss was to take myself on a retreat. I knew from my training as a therapist that mourning is very important when one has suffered a loss and I knew from my training as a spiritual teacher that it is essential to be with the experience in a way that is both honoring to those who passed and to myself. So I went to the coast of Maine to a seaside resort and created my own silent retreat that included massage therapy, a good bit of pampering and much time by the sea. The ocean in its vastness was very calming. I sat by the sea for endless hours, not speaking with anyone, writing in my journal and drawing sketches of paintings that I would make representing my feelings about these experiences. I also did a great deal of chatting with God and with my guides. Through this time, with their help, the unfathomable very slowly became the reality.

Many people in my family were afraid that I was depressed or even suicidal, but in fact, I was actively mourning throughout my retreat. I allowed myself the time to cry, to remember, to laugh, to rage, to speak to both my father and brother and to try to understand why they had chosen to leave me at this time. I traveled through a range of emotions that was both wonderful and exhausting. I ate little and I swam. I was kind and gentle to my physical body by giving it massage and comfort and I was very kind to my emotional body by giving it a place to have all the feelings that I needed to feel. I was also kind to my spiritual body, arguing with God about the loss, going through the classic stages of processing grief, eventually coming to a place of acceptance.

It was not an easy journey for I had never lost anyone this close to me before, and the loss of two significant members of my family at the same time was quite overwhelming. Either loss would have required a great deal of processing, but together it was quite a lot to bear. Creating my own retreat allowed me to move through my feelings with a small measure of grace. Many times that is the most we can ask for in such a situation.

During my period of loss, I also sat shiva in the Jewish tradition. Shiva is a period of one week during which you welcome visitors and they comfort you and bring you food. It is helpful to have this ritual, but it's not nearly enough. I am often asked what is an appropriate grieving time and my answer is always the same: when you are done grieving.

Recently I spoke to a small group. I recognized one of the women as someone who had come to hear me speak before. She was in her eighties but still vigorous; in fact, she owned a resort and managed it herself. I noticed that she wore a wedding ring on a chain around her neck and I asked her about it. She said that it kept her husband with her at all times, but that her daughter had asked her to take it off because she had worn it too long. She had been wearing it for eight years. Did I think it was too long, she wanted to know? I said, "Does it give you comfort? Does it help you in your grief?" She said that it did. I told her, "Then you haven't been wearing it too long, and don't let anyone decide for you when you are done grieving."

Personally, I believe that we return over and over again through reincarnation. I believe that there is an essential part of us, our soul, as we call it, which remains with us through each of these incarnations, growing and developing to eventually contain whatever is our version of perfection. It's often a source of great comfort, but not always, as when we are in the middle of something painful.

Whether or not you believe in reincarnation, it's important to think of the grieving process as naturally as you would think of the growth process or the healing process from surgery. In many ways, it is very similar. When a surgeon cuts you open and removes or fixes something in your body, your body is in shock and needs a great deal of time to absorb the meaning of what has been lost or deal with what has been repaired. You must find a way to change and rebalance without that which used to be a part of you. The same is true of grief. It is a surgery of your heart. A part of you is lost; a piece of your emotional landscape is removed. If you always had to look through the branches of a tree to see off in the distance, and that tree is no longer there, your whole vista has changed. When you lose someone you love, your vista changes also. You may have adjusted to a different vista, but it's in fact a different reality, and that adjustment takes time.

> **It's important to think of the grieving process as naturally as you would think of the growth process or the healing process.**

Maybe you don't want to go off to the coast of Maine to mourn. Maybe playing the songs that remind you of someone you've lost will quiet your soul and make them feel closer. In Tibetan Buddhism, when someone dies, the body is brought to the top of a mountain, cut into pieces and left for the predatory birds to eat. This practice is called "sky burial," often referred to as "giving alms to the birds." This might seem barbaric to us, but in a land where the ground is permafrost and fuel for cremation is scarce, isn't it as valid as artificially preserving someone's flesh and then burying that preserved flesh in the ground? The point is not that you do a particular ritual, but rather that you seek an expression of loss that fills your soul and that instead of ignoring the loss, you perform that ritual in whatever way comforts you and honors the one you have lost.

There are also losses that are not so easy to define. The loss of a relationship is a death in itself. The loss of a job is a kind of death also. We often judge ourselves when we lose these things, but perhaps we should be judging ourselves by how we deal with their loss. We cannot often control what we lose; we can only control our response to it.

I often draw upon Buddhist concepts for their clear rationality. Buddhism is not a religion as the Judeo-Christian view would define it, but rather a way of thinking about the world. If we are truly present in the moment, as Buddhist teachings suggest, we would accept grief as simply another experience, something of this moment and not a permanent state, and something that is important for our personal growth and evolution.

Sadness

And what about sadness? I feel that it's also something that is barely acknowledged in our culture. When we look at magazines, advertisements, movies or YouTube videos, we see people who are smiling, laughing and happy. Of course, we would all wish to be happy all of the time, but isn't sadness an integral part of being human? Isn't it true that humans are the only animals that shed tears? And don't we have a reaction to seeing someone else shedding tears?

If the world was perfect and we were perfectly balanced in our natures, we would accept everything that occurs in our life with equanimity. I would like to be that person, but I am not. I certainly suffer my share of sadness. All I ask is that we are not scorned for expressing this emotion. I think there are a lot of factors to blame for this attitude. One may be the American "can do" mentality, dictating that we must be tough and face whatever challenges that occur, and that it's okay to scoff about our problems, but not okay to cry if things are truly sad.

A theory of developmental psychology says that in order for a child to become a competent adult, she must have a significant challenge before the age of ten. This challenge needs to be significant enough so that the child has to master it herself and integrate it into her life. Some examples might be an illness, parental divorce or the loss of someone she loves; any of these things would be traumatic enough to require a child to develop mechanisms for coping. Of course, I would never recommend traumatizing a child, but I do believe that early difficulty makes for a sturdier adult, one who can cope better with life's inevitable problems.

I would ask you to incorporate sadness into your range of emotions, bless it and accept it. Sadness makes you human. Imagine a world where there is no sadness. It would be a world where there is no joy, because we live on a spectrum of emotions and that spectrum must run from ecstasy to agony. All are part of life. People often say to me, "So-and-so has a good life, they've had no challenges, they've had no difficulties. Why do I have all these problems in my life?" I have never met such a person. I don't know anyone who has not been challenged deeply just by living, by growing up, having a family, making a living, and suffering inevitable loss. No one is immune to these things.

Sadness is not an illness; it is part of the human condition. I would not give up my sadness. It allows me to feel the joy of my gladness.

Anger

Anger is often a negative expression of fear. We cry out to the sky, we shout at God, we want things to be different, when, in fact, we are afraid. Sometimes anger is easier to feel and express than pain. Again, I think there is a large cultural component to this attitude. Anger is considered an acceptable emotion; it's something that's expected, for example, when someone has been wronged or a situation is frustrating or threatening. A show of anger is expected. One would state the unfairness of the situation and make one's case. I would suggest that when you are angry to consider the fact that you may be expressing something deeper. Your anger may, in fact, be fear that the situation is out of control or that you are being challenged or that you won't be able to handle what is happening.

Negative emotions such as anger, rage and frustration create negative energy. If you look at someone's auric field when they are angry, you might see spikes of red coming out of their energy body. People can actually throw out energy and harm other people even if they don't intend to do so. These negative emotions can actually hurt others around them, without a fist being hurled.

As I mentioned, in the very early days of working with my teacher, he told me that if I could heal, I could harm. This made me quite upset and for a while he kept telling me that I was sending "arrows" at him. I argued that I was not angry and that I had no intention of harming him. One day, he stood up and moved across the room, saying he wasn't sitting in my line of sight. I asked him what he was doing and he said, "I can't take you shooting at me like this. I need to get out of your line of fire." That made me frustrated, and I did become angry. But I could not recognize my emotion for what it was. I thought I was still feeling frustrated and confused. Sometimes we aren't even able to label our feelings.

This story ends in a somewhat humorous way. My teacher was sitting in his chair when all of a sudden the window broke behind him. I asked, "What just happened?" He said, "You just broke the window." I thought he was kidding. We got up and saw all the glass outside on the ground. I had indeed broken the window. He laughed at me and said, "I'll be sending you the bill for that." This incident was a real lesson for me that energy can move powerfully when generated by powerful emotions. Don't think this isn't true for you. Your negative feelings and thoughts actually move the energy around you in such a way that they can harm others.

So what should we do when we are angry? The first thing to do is to recognize that it is anger. Identifying our feelings is very important. Then, when we realize that we are angry, we should begin a meditation or even a simple *pranayama* breath. Know that you can work with anger; the breath will help release it. Try the suggestions on the following page.

I believe that in trying to be in our "Buddha mind,"[8] we must feel the feelings that we have, even the negative ones. The real danger is *not* having feelings and not releasing them. In fact, we can become ill when they are repressed, internalized and dwelled upon in an unhealthy manner. That is not Buddha nature; that is illness. Would you have someone give up their joy? We ask for a rainbow in all things; we need to remember that we have a rainbow of emotions as well.

---

[8] "Buddha mind" is a term that describes the realization that life is suffering, but we can choose happiness despite it, walking a "middle way" of moderation with compassion for all living beings.

WORKING WITH ANGER

Take a deep breath. I believe in the "sleep on it rule." If I get mad enough that I feel like punching or screaming or doing something that might bounce back to me later, I sleep on it. If in the morning I still feel the same way, I will probably be able to express myself more articulately anyway.

Say it! If you still feel angry, tell the person. You may not be yelling after your night's sleep, but you can map out point-by-point how you feel and why. Quiet anger is very powerful. Think of the Godfather. Make them an offer they can't refuse.

If someone isn't worth fighting with, don't. We all know people who are just impossible to reason with. Don't waste your breath. Get out of the situation. They are bullies; let them bully someone else. You can't reason with someone who won't listen. You'll only experience a drain of your own energy.

Feel it! You may not be able to scream in the moment, but go home and punch a pillow or a punching bag. Or try my personal favorite, screaming in the car. The car is the best "screaming room." No one can hear you and it sounds really loud and satisfying. I do it a lot. So if you see someone screaming on the highway, it's probably me—give a wave!

Use your anger to get out of impossible situations rather than tolerate them. If your boss is always making you go home steaming, take that steam and get a new resume together. Use that to get yourself out and look for another job. Righteous indignation is great engine fuel.

Acknowledge, Accept, Release. This simple little mantra is the way to deal with strong negative emotions. We can learn to control our reactions and the impact that we have on others.

THE RIVER MEDITATION

For this exercise, please see the next chapter, "Surrender." The River Meditation is the best way I know to release negative emotions.

CHAPTER SIXTEEN

The Victory of Surrender

I don't know about you, but when I hear the word "surrender" the first thing that comes to mind is the scene in "The Wizard of Oz" where the wicked witch wrote in the sky in big green letters "SURRENDER DOROTHY." This is not the type of surrender we are talking about here. Surrender, to Dorothy, meant giving in to a terrible fate: being killed by the Wicked Witch of the West. But I believe surrender can be a positive and life-affirming choice.

I think the concept of surrender in western society is one that is almost always negative. It indicates losing a battle or giving in to a dark force. I would like you to turn that concept around and think about surrender in a positive way. I sometimes think that "surrender" should be the first chapter in this book. When we truly learn to surrender, we begin the first steps down our path to spiritual accomplishment and peace.

The way of surrender means accepting things that are not possible for you to change. The Serenity Prayer comes to mind: "God grant me the serenity to accept the things I cannot change; courage to change the things I can; and wisdom to know the difference."[9] That is the type of surrender we are talking about here, which includes the realization that there are things over which we have no control. It's hard to think of ourselves as powerless and I'm not asking you to do that. I'm merely asking you to acknowledge that there are powers and forces that are stronger and greater than you are. These powers and forces can be good or evil, or can be just a matter of being in the wrong or right place at any given time.

Surrendering can also mean listening to the divine voice, listening and taking its advice. We talked about this earlier when we learned about authentic voice. You can hear the true voice that is not your own narrative or monkey mind. When you listen to that voice and you comply, whether it is something you should do or something you should not do, that's the essence of surrendering. It means

[9] Part of a prayer attributed to Reinhold Niebuhr and adopted by Alcoholics Anonymous and other twelve-step programs.

acknowledging that you are not all-powerful. It can also be very liberating in that it allows you to let go of responsibility for everything that you cannot control.

The Illusion of Control

As I mentioned, several years ago I lost my brother. I don't think I really understood surrender until this happened. I spent a ridiculous amount of time thinking about all the things that I could have done to save his life: I could have been a better sister, I could have been a better healer, I could have recognized much sooner that his illness had progressed to the point that it had. Heck, I could have just moved the earth and moon and kept him from his fate and path! But I couldn't, because I can't live his life or his karma. A large part of the ability to surrender is understanding that we control no one's actions but our own. We really control no one's thought but our own. We don't even control our children's thoughts. We may be able to control their actions to some degree, but as anyone who has raised a child to adolescence knows, that's pretty much the end of the road for that issue.

When we truly learn to surrender, we begin the first steps down our path to spiritual accomplishment and peace.

After my brother died and I was completely alone with my thoughts and feelings, I did everything I could to understand what happened and whether I had a role in it. At the end of that time, I was able to surrender and say, "I could not have walked this path for him. I tried to help him in every way that I could. I loved him with all my heart and still do. He walked this path. I accept it. I don't like it, but I accept it. I surrender to you, God. I surrender to your knowing that you have taken him home to where he needed to go, perhaps to incarnate in another life to learn whatever lessons he did not complete here." Often the most difficult things to surrender are the things that we have absolutely no control over. So now when I feel that I'm taking on something that isn't mine, I actually invite myself to question: *Is this my problem? Is this something I need to solve? Is this something I have any control over?*

Here's another example. The current state and possible future of our planet can make many of us feel powerless. It drives me absolutely nuts that climate change is not being taken seriously. We may do everything we can to live consciously: try to eliminate plastic from our life, recycle most of everything we use, buy organically, write to Congress and ask them to change the laws, give money to environmental organizations. We may also try to educate others (sometimes to their great annoyance).

But ultimately, we have to surrender. Surrender does not mean that you give up on taking action, or that you forget about living your life in a way that is meaningful and right. At the end of the day we have to go to sleep in our own bed and be comfortable with who we are and our actions. That doesn't mean we are happy about global warming. But I know that I have to surrender—that this is something beyond my control and by letting it go, I can go on and do my work, have my life, laugh and be happy and have joy. If I held onto the responsibility for climate change, I would make myself insane. So surrender does not mean that you don't take action; it means that you accept the limitations of what you as an individual can do and turn the rest of it over to a higher power. It can be incredibly liberating.

Letting Go

I invite you to think about surrender in a new way. After you've done all the wonderful things you can do for yourself—you began meditation and prayer, you have implemented the things we've discussed in this book and you have followed the advice of your healthcare professionals and your spiritual counselors—there's a point where you just have to let it go. We are brought up to think that if we work hard enough and try hard enough, we will succeed. It's pretty much the American ethic, but it's not always the truth. Many people work diligently and never succeed and many people hardly work at all and succeed magnificently. I believe there is a karmic aspect involved. We can't change our karma; the plan that is out there for us is going to be there no matter what we do. So I would ask you to see surrender as a logical, restorative way to release your false sense of being in control and give you a new way of being in the world. If we can stop constantly comparing our past to our present, our past to our future, our present to our future, our neighbor's lawn to our lawn and just stay with what's going on right now, amazing things happen. There will be more on "the now" in the next chapter on living in the present moment.

I'm not a person who gives in easily to the concept of surrender. It took me many, many years to grasp this concept and implement it. It's something I'm far from perfect at. Every day in my prayers I ask to be able to surrender the day to whatever God or the universe wants me to do and has in store for me. If that means that I get a wonderful day with lots of fun things to do, that's terrific. But it might also mean I get a horrible day with lots of pain and suffering of others and myself. There was a song that goes something like this: "It's not what you look like when you're doing what you're doing/it's what you're doing when you're doing what it looks like you're doing." In a funny way, that sort of sums it up. That statement is probably more about the way someone is just comparing their looks to someone else, but the point is there. If you aren't living your life, nobody is. So let go.

What does letting go look like? It surely doesn't mean lying on the couch all day eating bonbons. It's knowing which things you have little or no power over, accepting them and being present with whatever you are feeling. It's dangerous to hold on to your emotions. Consider the idea of surrendering to your emotions. That doesn't mean having a temper tantrum when anything upsets you; it means that you acknowledge, *That's making me angry; I think I'm going to surrender to that feeling, let the feeling go through me and release it.* You experience what's going on but it doesn't take over and ruin your whole day. That is surrender. It doesn't mean don't try, but it does mean have some grace in the face of what's inevitable. You're going to screw some things up; you're going to behave badly. Other people will behave badly towards you and that's okay because we are all marching toward perfection. We're all trying to make that walk to Nirvana. And few of us are bodhisattva.[10]

When I began to study with my teacher, I would complain about my reactions to trivial things, expecting that if I was taking on a spiritual practice, I wouldn't be so reactive. He would often say to me, "Ah, you have become a bodhisattva and you didn't tell me? I wasn't invited to the party." He would laugh at me. And being young and foolish, I would get angry because he was laughing at me. My concern was extremely, supremely important and how dare he indicate that it wasn't? As was my nature, I had expected myself to behave perfectly in every situation and then questioned myself when I failed so miserably. I needed to learn how to surrender to the normal nonsense of daily life. I thought that it was never going to aggravate me when my children misbehaved, that I wouldn't scream at the cat when she threw up all over the rug—that I would be something that wasn't a human being! I needed to learn how to surrender.

I now set as a goal in my life that I will be in my Buddha consciousness for 85 percent of the time. No, I don't always achieve that, but I try. The other 15 percent is left over for gossip, silliness and just plain ornery behavior. So give yourself a break and try on the concept of surrender. It's really the key to having a spiritual life.

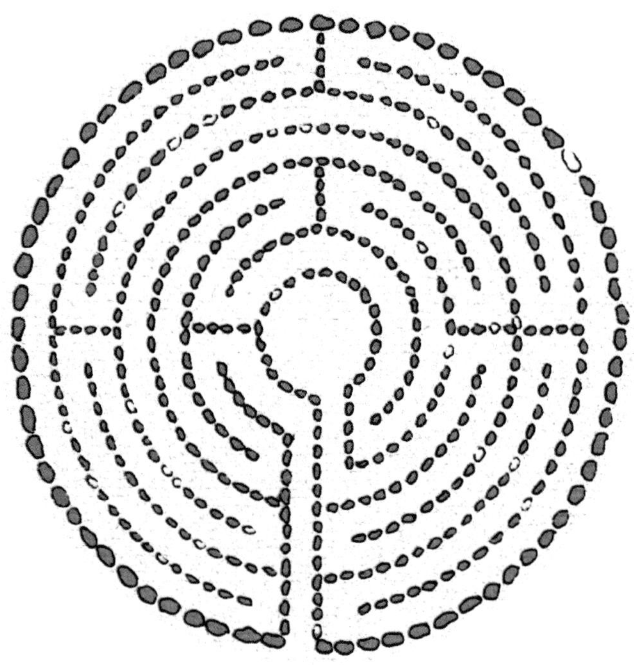

[10] A bodhisattva is one who is able to reach Nirvana (total freedom from suffering and delusion) but delays doing so out of compassion in order to save suffering beings.

THE RIVER MEDITATION

I'm going to teach you the River Meditation, which to me is the best way to release negative emotions. It is a powerful meditation, with many other names and variations. I think of it in fishing terms: it is the "catch and release" of emotions. Read through to see how it works and then find a quiet place to try it.

Assume a comfortable sitting position, making sure that your body is aligned and straight.

Begin counting the breath as we have learned, feeling your breath coming in and out of your body.

Now imagine yourself sitting by a river. It can be a river that you know in your dream world or one that you conjure up specifically for this purpose.

Find a comfortable place to sit by this river: a warm rock in the sun, a mossy or grassy area, whatever you wish. Get yourself really comfortable.

Notice the sky, the temperature, the trees, rocks and smells around you. Allow yourself to be fully present in this place.

Look into the water as it flows by you from left to right. Is it smooth and flowing or is it rapid and bubbly? It's your river, your place; you can make it whatever you like.

Now imagine that a craft comes down the river entering your field of vision from the left and stopping right in front of you. (My craft looks like Tom Sawyer's raft, but it can be anything; it can be a clipper ship if you'd like.)

Look at your vessel and see what emotion of yours it is carrying. If it is a negative emotion such as anger, sample it. Sampling means you allow yourself to "taste" and feel it for a moment, without getting into it. Do not engage the emotion; just allow yourself to recognize it. (For example, I was sad about my friend who was very ill. I could say "I'm feeling really sad about this illness and my helplessness to change it.")

Without engaging yourself, leave the emotion on the boat and release it off to the right to continue down the river.

Watch it until it is out of sight, perhaps meandering down, to finally disappear over the horizon.

(continued)

Then wait for the next vessel to come down and stop in front of you. It might be carrying a completely different emotion or the same emotion directed toward different people. For example:

The next emotion might be happiness. You just got a raise and you're glad. You will be able to do a lot more with that extra money. But for now you're just going to let the boat come by, notice your gladness and release it again down the river.

Repeat as many times as you need to. River Meditation can be done over and over again to release emotions.

You might wonder why we would wish to release positive emotion such as happiness. The answer is that the point of the exercise, the point of any meditation, is to create stillness, the silence that holds the mind in "neutral." It's not that we don't want to be happy, but we need the empty, silent space to just *be*. This is a major spiritual step.

I once taught this exercise to a teenage girl who was caught up in the drama of her emotional life to the point where it interfered with normal activities. I taught her this meditation and she seemed quite engaged with it. All of a sudden, she began laughing with great abandon. That's not usually the response that people have to this meditation so I asked her, "Why are you laughing?" She said that she had taken a rocket launcher and was blowing up each of the boats as they came by! Although that was a very original idea, for this meditation practice it really was quite the opposite of the intention. It makes for an amusing story, but the point is obvious. We are simply observing our emotions, acknowledging them and releasing them. This sounds easy but it's quite difficult to do; in fact, it is considered one of the more difficult meditations. Remember, the idea is to be an observer of your emotional state, not to be "in it."

Many variations exist on this meditation: the Ocean Meditation, the Wind Horse Meditation, etc., but it's basically the same thing. I've sat and done this meditation for long stretches of time. It was quite a revelation to me to find deeply buried things that I had some resentment or anger about, also feelings that I hadn't even thought about for years. It's an amazing and wonderful way to "house clean" emotions and I recommend it whenever necessary. It may not deal with some of your incredibly strong emotions or right when you're in the thick of them, but it's a good exercise to do regularly and on a long-term basis.

I encourage you to take fifteen minutes at the end of your day and release whatever emotions you are holding onto, surrender them, and let them be—let them leave you. Clean your internal house. Give it a try.

CHAPTER SEVENTEEN

Living in the Present Moment

There are only a few people who I would consider to be Enlightened Beings in this day and age. One of them is the Dalai Lama. Just think about his life: he was born into an extreme and unique life that he never wished for nor even thought about. Chosen at a very young age as an incarnation of the previous Dalai Lama, he may even be the last of his kind. He has chosen to separate from his political and legal rulership of Tibet and retain just his religious leadership.

Both modern man and antiquated concept, he has said so many profound and wonderful things with perhaps the most wonderful smile on the planet. His works have changed my life in significant ways. He is the one who got me to understand the concept of "living in the moment." Through listening to his teachings and reading his words, I have come to understand this central Buddhist concept. I've realized quite simply that it's the key to happiness.

It's Always Now

I've talked in other parts of this book about "monkey mind" or "running our personal loop." The monkey mind keeps us from living our life because we are focusing on past offenses, future riches and the like, and missing the joys that are right in front of us. Living in the moment means actually being in your body, mind and soul at this time no matter what you are doing. That can be swimming a lap, patting your dog, or simply breathing. Living in the moment is not at all easy to do, but it's very worthwhile.

When you hold on to anything from the past, especially bad events, they ache like a sore tooth and don't allow you to enjoy the dish of ice cream or the beautiful bird outside your window. You miss the joy in life by focusing on things that can't be changed, that have already been done. I'm not suggesting that you forget your past or your family history, or who you are and what you've done. You need to learn lessons from those things; who are we if not the sum total of the things that we have done in our lives? That's the difference between putting your life in context by viewing your history and perseverating about it. When you get stuck in a loop about the hurtful things that your sister said to you when you were kids or how your brother-in-law really was a jerk at that barbecue last month, you are wasting precious moments of your life that you can never get back. Do you really want to waste your time worrying about a barbecue when you could be thinking about the Divine or sipping a glass of scotch?

As for the future, planning is a good thing; anticipation of wonderful events is a good thing. I've always said that my favorite part of the weekend is Friday night because it is full of anticipation; the whole weekend is in front of me with all of the wonderful things that I'm going to do; I love savoring the possibilities. But if I only think about the future, if I think, *When I'm old enough to retire I won't have enough money because the economy is bad and my housing value has gone down and my kids and I can't make enough money to take care of me* and so on, I'm just running the loop forward, letting my monkey mind jump to the future rather than the past. What a waste of breath. What a waste of precious, precious time.

I often envy my cat. Her name is Freida Catlo. She is a very pampered being and deserves to be. She works with me in my office every day, sometimes comforting people, sitting on their feet, butting heads with them if they're sad and playing the fool when they need cheering up. Observe your cat if you have one. They are role models for living in the moment. They do not accept discomfort or unhappiness easily. If you try to brush them and they do not wish to be brushed, they will make their feelings quite clear and do everything in their power to get out of that situation. If they are happy they will show it; if they want attention paid to them or want their tummy scratched, they will come right up to you and demand it. They live in the present. Their joy is clear and apparent: they purr. Their displeasure is also clear and apparent: they meow or hiss. This is not to say that we should emulate our cats, but we can learn a valuable lesson from them.

Take several deep cleansing breaths and get back to your life, because your life is in these moments.

Staying in the present is difficult. It takes a concerted effort to get to a place where it's possible most of the time. I said earlier that I want to be in my bodhisattva nature 85 percent of the time. That's my goal. It's a very ambitious goal and I certainly don't always make it. I'm not above looking at someone on the street and thinking they need the fashion police or gossiping on occasion. But my goal is to remain in the present, experiencing what I am currently living with the greatest amount of joy I can muster. Sometimes all I can muster is pain, but whatever it is, it is Now. It is in real time.

If you try to practice being in the moment for a day, you'll find it's actually quite difficult. Every time you catch yourself ruminating about something that has happened or projecting something that's going to happen tomorrow, next week or next year, stop. Take several deep cleansing breaths and get back to your life, because your life is in these moments. There will be plenty of time to look back when we are no longer as capable as we are now, and I know with every fiber of my being that we'll deeply regret having wasted time either in the past or future because it will mean things that we never did, never saw and never accomplished.

PRESENT MOMENT

NOW IS THE DAY

Set aside a day when you are going to live in the present, just one day. It won't be easy, as we are constantly under pressure to think about the past and project into the future. Select a day when you can control, to the best of your ability, what's going to happen. This might be a day when you can be alone and have no plans—that's the perfect opportunity to practice remaining in the moment.

When you wake up, instead of jumping out of bed, rest for a moment, think about your dreams, feel the luxury of the sheets beneath you and the warm blanket above you. Stretch and feel each part of your body, become conscious of your toes and your knees and elbows and your ears. Allow yourself to be grateful for just being alive.

Feel your breath... Feel your breath again. And again. And realize that this act of breathing in and out has become automatic. Bringing it into your consciousness grounds you in the moment. So during the course of this very special day, stop every so often just to breathe and bring your awareness to your breath.

After you get out of bed, actually feel what it is like to brush your teeth and comb your hair. Don't do these things automatically, but allow them to be special and new as if you are seeing your hair for the first time, your teeth for the first time. Again, become conscious of your breath, what it feels like.

Jot down that you have done your daily maintenance. You may think, Oh my daily maintenance is boring and I want to rush through it as quickly as possible. *That's not being in the moment. It's possible to take pleasure from brushing your teeth, feeling that they're getting clean, brushing your hair, thinking,* My hair is so soft and wavy. I'm glad I have this nice soft wavy hair; it feels so nice to touch. *This self-talk may sound a little silly, but the act of noticing each of these things as they are occurring, although perhaps difficult to do, is essential to living in a healthy manner.*

If you can continue through your day noticing all your typical activities and stopping every half hour or so to breathe consciously and jot down notes about what you've done (on this day that you are "doing nothing"), you will see that you have done quite a bit.

(continued)

This experience can be very simple. Do this note-taking as close as you can to every half hour during the day. Your notes can be anything about your present experience: I feel cranky/hungry, look at that beautiful sky wow that's a big car—*whatever you observe about your inner and outer state. You won't be able to do this perfectly but do the best you can without reading it until the end of the day. At that time, you'll find that you had an amazing day full of beautiful experiences that you would have totally missed if you hadn't stopped to record them.*

We all know someone who walks around smiling all the time doing simple tasks. They're making their bed and are whistling a tune; they're brushing their teeth and smiling. They're walking the dog with a jaunty little step. These are people who, at least at that moment, are staying in the present time.

Think about what life would be like if you didn't have to stop and record your experiences but could be fully present for all of them. Wouldn't that be wonderful? You would be living your life.

The Next Steps on Your Journey

Your journey is just beginning. Thank you for allowing me to walk with you on your path. In this guidebook, we have explored many aspects of your spiritual life:

You now have a basic working knowledge of your energetic body, as well as some tools to help you set your moral compass towards Light Work. Not everyone will become a Lightworker, but hopefully you will consider the effects of each of your actions upon your life and going forward for many generations.

With your guides as allies and teachers, you have begun to listen to the authentic voice within and identify and honor your intuitive gifts. You have created a sacred space as your spiritual home. Remember that you always have a sacred space within you, a place of centered awareness from which to journey and learn.

As an energy sensitive person, you are now better equipped to protect yourself energetically in difficult environments and to clear challenging relationships both present and past. Remember also that while you can do much on your own, a spiritual teacher and a spiritual community may help you stay centered on your path and help through the inevitable difficult times.

Please remember that regular meditation, awareness and the cornerstones of practice described here serve to anchor your spiritual practice and to integrate and reinforce all that you have learned.

Make space for miracles and be grateful for the life force that enables you to be fully human and maybe a bit divine.

Both surrender and the present moment are concepts that I believe are key to a spiritual, successful and contented life. If you acknowledge and then empty yourself of the negative feelings and surrender to the things that you cannot change, then you are left with the present moment. It is ideally how you should live your human life, experiencing everything that happens to you, good and bad, and thoroughly being there for it all.

Just as "everyone is our mother," everyone, every experience is our teacher. How else can you learn patience and compassion but through challenge? Growing these qualities is indeed the way to become a more compassionate person who can plant the seeds of a peaceful planet.

My hope is that you will take what you have learned and forge your path, unique and beautiful in its own way. That is what I wish for you all.

Namaste,
Wendy Marks

Further Reading

SPIRITUALITY AND RELIGION

Baldwin, William J. and Fiore, Edith. *Spiritual Releasement Therapy: A Technique Manual.* Headline Books.

Carroll, James. *Constantine's Sword: The Church and the Jews, A History.* Mariner.

Dalai Lama, His Holiness and Cutler, Howard, M.D. *The Art of Happiness: A Handbook for Living.* Riverhead.

Kamenetz, Rodger. *The Jew in the Lotus: A Poet's Rediscovery of Jewish Identity in Buddhist India.* Harper One.

Karpinski, Gloria D. *Barefoot on Holy Ground: Twelve Lessons in Spiritual Craftsmanship.* Ballantine.

Melody. *Love is in the Earth: A Kaleidoscope of Crystals.* Earth Love Publishing.

Singer, Michael A. *The Untethered Soul: The Journey Beyond Yourself.* New Harbinger Publications.

Sivananda, Swami. *All About Hinduism.* Divine Life Society.

Tolle, Ekhart. *The Power of Now: A Guide to Spiritual Enlightenment.* New World Library.

ANIMAL GUIDES, PERSONAL TOTEM POLE

Andrews, Ted. *Animal Speak: The Spiritual and Magical Powers of Creatures Great and Small.* Llewellyn Press.

Gallegos, Eligio Stephen, Ph.D. *The Personal Totem Pole: Animal Imagery, the Chakras and Psychotherapy.* Moon Bear Press.

SHAMANISM

Achterberg, Jeanne. *Imagery in Healing: Shamanism and Modern Medicine.* Shambhala.

Ingerman, Sandra. *Soul Retrieval: Mending the Fragmented Self.* Harper One.

Scott, Gini Graham. *The Complete Idiot's Guide to Shamanism.* Alpha.

Tredlock, Barbara, Ph.D. *The Woman in the Shaman's Body: Reclaiming the Feminine in Religion and Medicine.* Bantam.

INTUITION

Robinson, Lynn A. *Divine Intuition: Your Inner Guide to Purpose, Peace, and Prosperity.* Jossey-Bass.

Robinson, Lynn A. *Trust Your Gut: How the Power of Intuition Can Grow Your Business.* Kaplan.

HEALING AND MEDICINE

Breiner, Mark A., DDS. *Whole Body Dentistry: A Complete Guide to Understanding the Impact of Dentistry on Total Health.* Quantum Health Press.

Brennan, Barbara Ann. *Hands of Light: A Guide to Healing Through the Human Energy Field.* Bantam.

Bruyere, Rosalyn L. *Wheels of Light: Chakras, Auras, and the Healing Energy of the Body.* Touchstone.

Frawley, Dr. David. *Ayurvedic Healing: A Comprehensive Guide.* Lotus Press.

Santorelli, Saki. *Heal Thyself: Lessons on Mindfulness in Medicine.* Bell Tower.

Siegel, Bernie, M.D. *Love, Medicine and Miracles: Lessons Learned About Self-Healing from a Surgeon's Experience with Exceptional Patients.* William Morrow.

Weil, Andrew, M.D. *Spontaneous Healing: How to Discover and Enhance Your Body's Natural Ability to Maintain and Heal Itself.* Ballantine.

MEDITATION / MUSIC

Audio

Bharati, Swami Jnaneshvara. *Yoga Nidra Meditation: Extreme Relaxation of Conscious Deep Sleep.* Tranquility Productions.

www.Hemi-sync.com

www.soundstrue.com

Books

Lonegren, Sig. *Labyrinths: Ancient Myths and Modern Uses.* Gothic Image Publications.

Artress, Lauren. *Walking a Sacred Path: Rediscovering the Labyrinth as a Spiritual Practice.* Riverhead.

Made in the USA
Charleston, SC
02 April 2015